Thinking Out Loud on Paper

Thinking Out Loud on Paper

The Student Daybook as a Tool to Foster Learning

Lil Brannon
Sally Griffin
Karen Haag
Tony Iannone
Cynthia Urbanski
Shana Woodward

HEINEMANN • PORTSMOUTH, NH

Heinemann

A division of Reed Elsevier Inc.
361 Hanover Street
Portsmouth, NH 03801–3912
www.heinemann.com

Offices and agents throughout the world

The authors and publisher wish to thank those who have generously given permission to reprint borrowed material:

Excerpts from *Using the Workshop Approach in the High School English Classroom* by Cynthia Urbanski. Copyright © 2005. Published by Corwin Press. Reprinted with permission of the publisher.

Library of Congress Cataloging-in-Publication Data
Thinking out loud on paper : the student daybook as a tool to foster learning / Lil Brannon . . . [et al.].
        p. cm.
    Includes bibliographical references.
    ISBN-13: 978-0-325-01229-2
    ISBN-10: 0-325-01229-6
    1. Teaching—Aids and devices. 2. School notebooks. 3. Diaries—Authorship. 4. Creative thinking. 5. Creative writing. I. Brannon, Lil.

LB1044.88.T54 2008
371.33—dc22   2007039802

Editor: Jim Strickland
Production: Lynne Costa
Cover and text designs: Jenny Jensen Greenleaf
Cover photograph: Cindy Urbanski
Typesetter: Kim Arney
Manufacturing: Steve Bernier

Printed in the United States of America on acid-free paper
12   11   10   09   08   VP   1   2   3   4   5

CONTENTS

ACKNOWLEDGMENTS

This book comes out of our experiences in the National Writing Project. The University of North Carolina (UNC) Charlotte Writing Project brought us together and has sustained our work over the years. We are particularly indebted to Sam Watson, who founded the UNC Charlotte Writing Project, directed it for many years, and whose commitment to writing and teaching still animates the UNC Charlotte Writing Project and much of the thinking in this book. The book would not be possible without the gentle guidance and patience of our editor, Jim Strickland, whose work in English education is also present in what we say. Our students have given us their words, their images, and their excitement for learning with us. It is for them that this book is written. We thank them for their love of learning and for making our classrooms places of excitement and possibility.

Introducing the Daybook

It is not a bad idea to get in the habit of writing down one's thoughts. It saves one having to bother anyone else with them.

—Isabel Colegate

The daybook is a tool that we use in our daily lives with our students, as teacher researchers, as writers. It's the tool we use to muse over and investigate whatever is going on. It's a tool we use to learn and discover with our students.

As teachers, our goal is to empower our students and provide them with ways of learning that work best for them. Daybooks have helped us foster ways of learning that allow students the space and freedom to be silly and messy, to be thinkers and writers just for the sake of thinking and writing, to be miners of their thoughts even if just to dig out a golden line from something that they read.

The results are clear—we find that our students are successful in class, are prepared for tests or the next grade level, and, more importantly, are empowered by the joy of thinking and learning. Questions such as "why do I have to do this" are replaced by "listen to what I just wrote in my daybook." When this happens, we know we've done our job.

This book is not one of those programs that "come from the mountain top" that make you wonder, "how long is this gimmick going to last?" And it's not a book about writer's notebooks or how to organize your teaching life. This is a book about a tool for lifelong learning: the daybook. The daybook is different from a writer's notebook because it collects more than what might be used in a writing workshop, though you can use it there if you like. The daybook breaks down the typical disconnect that occurs in schools: disconnects between theory and practice, between one grade and the next, between one subject and another, and between the way people really learn and how we often feel obligated to make our students learn in very specific and predetermined ways.

Why Call It a Daybook?

Jim Burke (2007) has something he calls a daybook, which is his method of getting organized. We see Jim's daybook as a helpful tool that helps us plan instruction in a logical way, in much the same way as we like to keep our desks neat and tidy. Though we do use daybook planners to reflect on and plan instruction, our view of daybooks is more like our closets than our desks—a place where we store things, throw things into when friends are coming over, stuff with the junk of our daily lives, and, every now and then, clean out in order to find something worth presenting to someone else. Daybooks for us are thinking tools. As teachers we use them throughout our day to reflect and to research, and we ask our students to use them in our classrooms to research and think about their worlds.

The daybook, as we understand it, has a long history. Back in the fifth century BC, Protagoras, a sophist, kept records of important arguments and key concepts that were otherwise only preserved in memory. These records were called "commonplace books," and they were used from the classical period through the nineteenth century as a valuable tool for educating young minds. *Commonplacing* required students to enter important passages from literature and at times comment on those passages. In the seventeenth century, these books were known as *silva rerum* ("a forest of things"). These forests held beautiful passages and important arguments that could be called upon to apply to many different situations. People were considered truly knowledgeable if they could remember and quote important passages from their commonplace book (Knoblauch and Brannon 1984).

More directly, we take the term *daybook* from Donald Murray, who kept a daybook throughout his writing. In 1986, he gave this advice to scholars in rhetoric and composition:

> Keep a planning notebook with you to play in at the office, at home, in the car, or the airplane, at faculty meetings (especially at faculty meetings), while you're watching television, sitting in a parking lot or eating a lonely lunch. . . . The notebook, which I call a daybook, will make it possible for you to use fragments of time, and fragments of time are all that most of us really have. Fifteen minutes, ten, five, two, one, less. In this book you can make lists, notes, diagrams, collect the quotes and citations, paste in key articles and reference, sketch outlines, draft titles, leads, endings, key paragraphs that will make it possible for you to be ready to write when you have an hour, or two, or three clear. (148)

Our daybooks draw from this rich history; we ask students to use them to write about their lives, to keep track of their thinking, and to notice all the world around them with open eyes and ears and hearts. In our daybooks, there's all kinds of writing that just doesn't fit anywhere else: bumper sticker slogans that got us laughing when we were waiting at a stoplight (one Lil saw last week was, "Huked on Foniks reely worked fur me"); pieces of language that moved us (one golden line that Cindy loved is, "We grow into new selves with every sentence we write, with every choice we make among the almost endless set of possibilities for their construction. To fail in that articulation is to foreclose on our identities, to cut short the process of discovering ourselves in thought" [Imbrie 1999]). Day books have become a valuable tool in our classrooms—we want to share that learning and excitement with you.

What Grade Levels Are Daybooks Right For?

Each of us has taught either elementary school, middle school, high school, or college, and some of us have taught a combination of all the above. (Lil, Sally, and Cindy have taught middle, high school, and college students; Karen has taught elementary, middle, high school, and college students; Tony has taught elementary and college students; Shana has taught high school and college students.) When we taught in college for the first time, we all had almost the exact same experience. While we were home in the quiet of our studies, as the first day approached, we thought, "What am I doing?" We became so nervous at the prospect of teaching nineteen-year-olds that we stayed awake all night. Finally, at about two in the morning, we had an idea. If we could just write down what we would do for the first two weeks of class, we knew we would be well on our way. The plans we all wrote looked very much like what we had written for our elementary, middle, or high school students. The plans were driven by a common goal of helping our students realize that they are writers. No matter the age or grade level of our students now, the way we approach writing instruction in our classrooms from the first day is by having students think, write, and reflect. All of this thinking, writing, and reflecting is captured in our daybooks.

From this shared experience, we knew that the ways we teach writing, from fourth grade to college composition, were not that different. We knew as teachers that all of our students are writers, and their needs are very similar. Whether in the college or the seventh-grade classroom we had students who hated to write and students who had filled a couple dozen journals. In fourth grade or twelfth, we all had students who needed us a lot and students we would not get to know at all. In our sixth-grade classroom we had students whose thoughts were as deep as any high school student we had taught. And in our college classes we had some interesting "middle-grades thinkers." So we have found ideas from across the spectrum of grades helpful in meeting the needs for all the learners in our classes. With a bit of tweaking, what works for college students can and does also work for elementary children.

Cindy will tell you that she has learned more about teaching reading and writing for high school students from Karen's and Tony's elementary classrooms than anywhere else. Shana says maybe it's because teachers of older children assume too much about what kids already know. Cindy used to think it was because elementary teachers weren't as pressured by content, but Tony and Karen have shown her that their pressures are just as heavy, not to mention they've got all subject areas to deal with.

Karen and Tony will tell you they learn a lot by hanging out with middle, secondary, and college teachers. They like to talk theory and find the validation and the sources that support their teaching practices. Karen and Tony always take any high school or college classroom idea and instantly transform it to what will work with their school children. They always say, "My kids can do that!" Conversely, they like seeing how what they are doing with second or fourth graders is adapted by teachers of upper grades.

We develop as teachers by learning from each other. We invite you to join us by reading this book in whatever way works best for you. One strategy is to read straight through to the end, which is the best way to take in the wide range of our teaching experiences, grade levels, and the theory our practices are based on.

Use the internarrative connection boxes—the 4–6 Connection Box, the 6–12 Connection Box, and the 4–12 Connection Box—to help you adapt the ideas to the grade level you are currently teaching.

If you feel overwhelmed with the business of teaching, however, below are some other strategies to help you parse through some of the book's content and get you started with daybooks. We know that once daybooks become a part of your classroom, you'll find yourself returning to the book to learn more about them. The most important thing is for you to get started.

- Read through the practices and save the theory, denoted in shaded theory boxes, for reference or to enlighten a misguided administrator who questions what you are doing.

- Follow the strand for the level you teach. Just look for the name of the person you've connected with in each chapter. As you read what they have to say, you will find them pointing to other authors/teachers in the book.

Who Are We?

We came together as teachers of writing in the UNC Charlotte Writing Project, a site of the National Writing Project. Writing is what brought us together, and writing is what has kept us together, sharing our classrooms and our teaching. This book invites you into our community of writers and teachers to learn and share with us about how writing can become a valuable tool for learning and exploring and for having those thoughts visible for reflection and analysis.

Lil began her career in 1973 as a middle and high school English teacher in rural Celeste, Texas, population 719. She taught eighth-, eleventh-, and twelfth-grade English and coached junior high and high school girls basketball. She only tells her good friends about her coaching gig, because she doesn't want anyone to know that she had the state championship high school, class B team. In Texas, she is probably the only winning coach in the entire state not to become a principal. She became a college professor instead. She has spent the last twenty-five years working with teachers on teaching writing. She has worked in North Carolina and New York State, with teachers in the New York City Writing Project and the Capital Area Writing Project at the University at Albany, State University of New York, and now she directs the UNC Charlotte Writing Project.

Cindy started teaching in 1996 and managed to coach cross-country early on. As a beginning teacher she was totally focused on the North Carolina tenth-grade writing test, relishing in the report card at the end of the year, and drilling students mercilessly to ensure that the writing said exactly what she wanted it to say. After three years of writing all of her students' work for them in five perfectly formed paragraphs, she was exhausted. Lil made her come to the UNC Charlotte Writing Project, and this experience kept her teaching. In the Writing Project Cindy discovered daybooks and got so reenergized that she wanted to pull strangers off the street into her living room so that she could teach them to write in new ways. In the Writing Project she discovered that she needed to throw out everything she was doing in the English classroom, and bring in all the hands-on, experiential activities she learned from coaching cross-country. She needed to roll up her sleeves and get down and dirty with her students as writers.

Since 1974, Karen has taught in elementary schools, middle and high schools, and the college classroom. Currently, she is a literacy coach at an urban elementary Title I school. She joined the writing project in 1985, kicking and screaming, because she couldn't imagine spending five weeks writing. She didn't see herself as a writer. The experience of writing and of being in a community of dedicated teachers changed her life. She changed the way she viewed the goals of teaching. Before the Writing Project she valued the *products* her students created and gave little thought to learning that occurs throughout the *process*. The Writing Project helped her look at the child and value each child's path for reaching curricular goals. She also began to see herself as a researcher, talking to her students, asking them what worked and what needed work, and using their responses to change her lessons to better meet their needs. In 1993, she became a literacy coach, applying the same principles that she used with children to helping teachers.

Tony was badgered every year for more than ten years by Karen to become involved in the Writing Project. Tony was a social studies guy, and he loved making the world and social issues come alive to his fourth graders. Summers for Tony were spent working on new social studies activities and working with teachers to make social studies more important in the elementary school classroom. In 2002, Tony caved. He decided it was time to get Karen off his back and see what all this writing stuff was about. He got turned on to writing, returned to school with his Sponge Bob daybook, and now has his children writing throughout the curriculum. Social studies has never been so good.

Sally began her career as a writer, a reporter for a small-town newspaper in North Carolina. Teaching is her second career, one where she brings her love of writing into the lives of hundreds of high school students each year. Don't ask her about them unless you have an hour or two to spare. She will show you each one's latest endeavor (all one hundred of them) that she has saved for posterity on her jump drive (that is, if she can find her jump drive). Sally is always ahead of the curve. She was blogging with her students when the rest of us were still using our Commodore 64s; her students were producing movies when the rest of us were trying to figure out how to make points fly in PowerPoint. Now that she's approaching retirement, she's channeling some of her creative energy into completing a Ph.D.

With a background in high school English education and a Master's degree in English, Shana is the youngest of the group, but she is wise beyond her years (or at least we let her think she is). Whether preparing tenth-grade students for the writing test, helping seniors apply for college, or introducing college freshmen to the rigors of postsecondary education, Shana has been immersed in the teaching of writing. So, when she started her Ph.D. in Literacy and English Education, getting involved with the UNC Charlotte Writing Project was a no-brainer. Calling upon her teaching and coaching skills (Shana also played college soccer and coached high school and college), she approaches the teaching of writing with passion and encourages leadership in her classroom. The Writing Project has provided her with a theoretical knowledge and a network of teachers she needed to pursue her desire to rethink the way writing is taught in kindergarten through college.

Some of Our Encounters with Daybooks

▶ Lil

In the summer of 1981, when I first team-taught a course with James Britton, I noticed that he carried with him a small 3-by-5-inch notebook that he could slip into his pocket. At dinner one night, I asked him, "Jimmy, what is that you are carrying?"

"Oh, this is my daybook."

"Your what?"

"My daybook. Look. I make notes throughout my day, notes about everything, where I am, what I'm doing, things people say. It's a way for me to keep track and to think about things that matter to me. It gives me a history to return to. In one of my daybooks I have a note about receiving a call from Gordon Pradl. He was at Harvard at that time, and had read some of my work. That call changed the course of my academic life. My daybook allowed me to record that moment. And now, I treasure returning to those thoughts. What I'm interested in right now are my interactions with my granddaughter. I record things she says and does, just as I record things that are happening in our class. You'll see some of those stories in my academic work to come."

I did see how Jimmy was able to use his daily encounters with his grand-daughter to illustrate his theory of writing, how it moves from the expressive, from that language that is close to ourselves, the language we think in, to what Jimmy called the transactional, the more academic and public discourses we teach in school.

▶ *Cindy*

When I was in high school and college, I was drawn to those pretty flowered journals that they sold in bookstores. I couldn't leave a store without purchasing one, and I would spend days imagining how neat it would be to write wonderfully profound thoughts that would live long after I was dead. That image made it to-tally impossible to write anything. When I would try anyway, my thoughts were messy, nothing that I would want anyone to see at any time, much less after I was dead. When I got over trying to be profound and would talk just about my life, I would live in fear that my parents or one of those stuck up girls in third period would find my journal and tease me mercilessly.

This was my pattern until graduate school where I was introduced to the day-book. The daybook was a messy, unorganized, free-for-all of thought, a place to stick and glue in the scraps of stuff I would accumulate—quotes, comic strips, postcards. And I didn't have to worry about anyone but me reading it. No one else would want to. At first I kept my daybooks in those pretty spiral notebooks, and I would take great pleasure in scribbling messily in it. I remember one day when Lil asked me, "How do you use that thing? I would be afraid I would mess it up." I showed her how I would scribble and not write at all on the lines. The lines were too far apart.

Daybooks quelled my fears. Losing the fear, the fear of others seeing my mess and the fear of making mess, freed me to be a writer.

▶ *Shana*

When I first started working with Cindy and Lil in the Writing Project, I wanted to keep my daybook on my laptop. I wanted to be efficient. I wanted to maximize my time and effort. I had goals: Write to publish; be right from the start. I re-member asking Cindy, "Would it be OK for me to use my laptop for in-class writ-ing instead of this composition book?" I was thinking, "how high school is this—a composition book for writing." Cindy said gently, "Please try the composition book for a couple of weeks. Write there. Feel free to be messy, to slow down, to be quiet with yourself. We can revisit this after you give it a try." We never had to revisit the issue. There was something powerful about writing and thinking on paper, of having a place to write badly, to be inefficient, rambling, and unorganized.

Now that you know our stories, grab a pen and a composition notebook, read on, and create your own daybook encounters.

2

From Workbook to Working Book

Writers write. They use writing throughout their day. They use writing to learn, to think, and to feel. Writing is like breathing. Writers can't live without writing.

—LIL BRANNON

A Tale of Two Classrooms

Once upon a time, students sat in rows at desks in a classroom. Typically, the students would hunch over their workbooks grasping number-two pencils. "Who is the main character?" a student wondered; she had to answer ten questions about the story. "The main character is . . ." she wrote, dutifully remembering to write in complete sentences. She yawned as she lazily scrawled a period at the end. The classroom was absolutely silent. She looked around. Nine more questions to go.

Another student sat puzzling over the directions in his workbook. "Write about a time you confused right with left," the prompt read. The student stared at the blank page. He looked at the clock. He had absolutely nothing to say about this topic. In fact, he cared nothing about the topic at all. The school district bought this workbook for every child. Many pages were not filled in, not because the boy hadn't done the work, but because the teacher had neither the time to assign nor to read all the workbook pages. The teacher only had time to feel guilty as she circled the room to make sure everyone was completing the assignments. "Perhaps, they will complete the pages over the summer," the teacher thought, trying to justify the cost of the workbooks.

Contrast that classroom to a very different classroom: A quick scan of the room reveals desks grouped together, creating tables. There's a hum of voices as children go about their work. Some sit on the floor with a partner or two eagerly sharing what they wrote about last night. Others read and prepare for discussion groups. They mark the reading with sticky notes so that they will remember their observations and/or questions for reflective writing later. Some students write double entry journals, like notice/wonder charts, to remember their thoughts when their discussion group gets together. Each student searches for clues that might reveal what is going to happen in the book she is reading or a theory about why the author wrote the book in the first place.

The students lean over to one another to get help when they are stuck. The teacher meets with small groups of students every day teaching them how to read, write, talk, recognize their thinking, and listen to one another. Mostly, she observes carefully and takes cues from the students. All of this thinking, reflecting, problem posing, and discovery gets recorded safely into her daybook—a journal of sorts, but with a *big* difference.

What Is a Daybook?

We think of the daybook like that drawer in the kitchen where we stick everything that does not yet have a place, but we know we might need someday. It's not quite trash, but it is the leftovers, the twist ties, the artifacts of where we have been. The daybook serves as a place where students put all of their thoughts throughout the day. It isn't a binder with sections. It isn't even a binder. We use an old-fashioned composition notebook because it is cheap, has a hard cover, and its pages stay put. Before daybooks, our students often misplaced their work. Now, the daybook serves as a collection place to keep everything, and we mean *everything*. Discussions and lessons grow out of the practice students do and the questions students ask, all of which are recorded in their daybooks.

A daybook needs to be a hardcover notebook with stitched-in pages. It needs the hard cover so students can bring it back and forth from home to school and keep it in useable shape. A daybook with pages that are difficult to rip out forces students to gradually let go of the perfectionism they have learned to expect of themselves. They learn to accept pages that don't work. With help, they view mistakes as potential successes. Drafts that turn out to be lists, for example, can be viewed as a dozen possible story ideas. In order to capture the true essence of a daybook, we discourage our students from using spiral notebooks, three-ring binders, or fancy, expensive, easily damaged journals. By sticking to these guidelines, teachers and students don't have to worry about spiral-bound journals locking together when they all are stacked in one place, or pages coming loose, binders becoming bent, or the avalanche that inevitably happens when anyone tries to pick up more than three binders at a time.

Why Daybooks Work

In *Jazmin's Notebook*, Nikki Grimes writes, "It seems like ideas are like gossamer, or mist, fragile as a dream, forgotten as soon as you awake" (1993, 25). But with daybooks, ideas don't get scattered and lost any more. One daybook can bring organization to a writer's life, even a messy, disorganized writer. The daybook differs from a journal in that the daybook includes much more than just the students' personal and often private thoughts.

Like writers' notebooks, daybooks are a place for students to store all of their writing on the way to creating a final product. But they also keep in their daybooks math problems, social studies questions, and their private thinking about what happened at lunch. Students need this place to hold onto the thoughts and notes they discover throughout their entire day, not just the time they are in English class. So daybooks are not just for writing—they integrate all subjects. They are often messy and filled with incomplete pages. Many daybooks have colorful sticky notes marking important pages. Some students divide their notebooks into chapters, but they don't have to. Also, we usually don't write to the students in their daybooks, and more importantly, we don't grade the writing in the daybook but we do check to see that students are doing their work. (See more on assessment in Chapter 7.)

Ralph Fletcher explains his writer's notebook in this way: "Most of what goes into a notebook defies description. Labeling it, well, stuff, is about as close as you

The Daybook: A Student's Process of Learning

A daybook captures students' thinking, making it visible to them. We often tell our students that the writing in their daybooks is their "thinking out loud on paper." We say we aren't so much concerned with the quality of their writing but with the quality of their learning. The daybook is a student's process of learning. James Britton, in his essay "Language and Learning Across the Curriculum," says that writing of this kind is useful for teachers who already understand that learning isn't uni-directional; that is, learning isn't the students writing down what the teacher says. Learning is interactional and social in nature. Teachers and students learn together, or as Britton says, "Knowledge is a process of knowing rather than a storehouse of the known" (1983, 221).

When we shift our focus from *product* to *process*, the daybook becomes an essential tool for learning. Lev Vygotsky (1978), a Russian psychologist, claims that students develop as writers when they are using writing to fulfill some need that lies outside the act of writing itself. Much the way infants learn to speak in order to understand and be understood, young writers learn to write by making sense of their world and communicating that understanding to themselves and others. Writers, therefore, need to write often so that they make their thinking—their processes of thought—apparent to themselves.

can get. If your notebook is like mine, it will fill up with stuff you can't quite live without" (1996, 25). A daybook is just stuff, the stuff of a child's day, the stuff that she will return to as a reader, writer, and thinker.

The view of writing discussed in the Theory Box above is very different from more traditional purposes of writing in schools, in which students write down what the teacher says or copy notes from the board, and where writing is more "fill in the blanks" or "follow the formula" than it is thinking and learning. A daybook won't work well in a traditional classroom because there is no purpose for it. A daybook works in classrooms that are concerned with what and how children learn and where teachers are curious about what and how children think.

Donald Murray, from whom we have already acknowledged our debt for the idea of a daybook, writes that his "students become writers at the moment when they first write what they do not expect to write" (1982, 3). "Writers," for Murray, "seek what they do not expect to find. Writers are like artists, rationalizers of accident. They find out what they are doing after they have done it" (1982, 4). Instead of knowing in advance what their topic sentence is, students discover what they want to say in the process of saying things. Many writers have this experience, and Murray collected those writers' experiences in *Shoptalk* (1990). For example,

I'm working on something, I don't know exactly what. (115)
—EUDORA WELTY

Inch by inch the words surprised me. (105)
—WILLIAM KENNEDY

In order for a daybook to matter in teaching and learning, teachers and students must come to terms with what it means to be a writer. If writing and thinking were easy, we wouldn't struggle as teachers with how to help our students find their voices as writers. Daybooks can become *working books*, where teachers and students work out their ideas and think and explore their worlds. Teachers must give class time for writing, knowing that when they do so they are giving class time for thinking. Teachers must give class time to share bits and pieces of this writing, so that everyone can hear how a writer thinks or feels or makes sense of experience. In doing so, teachers and children begin to understand that they are writers.

Daybooks have been our way to make our classrooms a community of writers. Karen's story, which follows, shows how she moved from notebooks to daybooks, making her classroom come alive with writing.

Karen's Story: A Teacher Writer Discovers Daybooks

A skeptic, I was reluctant to try a daybook. I was a three-ring notebook kind of girl. Ripping out pages, moving pages around, and hole-punching papers to add to my binder worked for me. I liked writing on a thick stack of lined paper with just the right pen. Wadding up papers and arching them into the garbage can like I'd seen writers do on television helped me do my best work. At the time, I was not writing for myself either. I was only doing the writing that I was required to do as a teacher, the icky, boring stuff.

As I began to write for myself, I discovered I enjoyed the smallness of the daybook and how it fit in my bag. It traveled with me easily. Having it with me helped me jot down ideas as they occurred to me. As I experimented with my new daybook, I felt the freedom of not worrying about mistakes, not crossing out ideas or throwing away pages. The fact that the pages were stuck in a bound composition book required that I hold on to all this material. What I discovered was that with the binder, I tossed away ideas that could actually have become a part of other writings. Or perhaps what I found was that with the daybook, my writing could grow out of the little bits and pieces of many different days. I felt free to experiment with my writing by writing in different colors, in the margins, and sideways. After all, it was my daybook and I wasn't showing it to anyone.

Thoughts came to me while watching television, riding in the car and at school, eating breakfast or brushing my teeth. My ideas didn't get lost anymore because my daybook was close at hand. On the rare occasion when I left it at home or at school, I felt uncomfortable. I learned to write on scraps of paper and then glue them onto the pages when my daybook and I were reunited. When I thought of a story idea, I would jot it down in the back of my daybook. I realized that I began turning to the *last* page because I could locate it quickly. The last page became my topic list.

I also began inventing solutions to my writing problems. I labeled ideas I wanted to come back to with quickly drawn clouds that I could spot as I flipped through the pages of my daybook. I still wanted to give students handouts, and I wasn't sure how to incorporate these pages into a composition book (the binder did work well for these materials). My resolution was to fold the page in half, run a glue stick down both sides of the folded edge, and then stuff the fold of the paper inside my notebook. I closed my daybook and pressed on the binding. The handout stuck so well, I could pick up my daybook by holding the glued-in sheet.

As my daybook grew fat, I realized how important it would be to invite my students to keep a daybook as well. As we started to work together, I shared with my students all the tricks I had discovered, such as the clouds I put around great ideas, the pasted in pieces that I didn't want to lose. As all our daybooks grew, we found it difficult to locate the next fresh page quickly. So, we started using a rubber band as a bookmark or a sticky note to label places we needed to find quickly. The rubber band also became a great place to hook a pen, so we could have our favorite pens with us at all times as well.

Once I attempted to make sections for our daybooks but gave up on that. The stick-on dividers worked fine, but I couldn't guess how many pages we might need for each section. Also, I couldn't figure out what chapters worked consistently. So instead, we started simply dating everything instead of fussing with divisions. (Lil uses the same colored sticky notes on pages that might work or feed into something she is writing—yellow stickies are ideas that go with a workshop she is preparing, pink stickies go with a grant application she is working on. They are like dividers with a difference; instead of pages being all together, they are linked by the rainbow of colors.)

When my first daybook ran out of pages and I started my second, I knew I needed some way to keep track of the pages that really mattered to me, such as a table of contents to make it easier to revisit my ideas. I numbered the pages in the upper corners and made a list of the pages that really mattered to me, or that

I looked at from time to time. Locating what I needed by flipping the pages with my thumb was easy when the pages were numbered and catalogued.

About this same time, I began writing more on the computer. Moving from pen to type meant I had less in my daybook, and I went many months without using it. Then I realized I missed my daybook: I still needed a place to take notes and to catch thoughts when away from my desk. I also found it invaluable for revising—if I were stuck at my computer, I'd locate my daybook, find a fresh page, and freewrite revisions. Breaking away from the computer helped me find my way through my writing. I also looked forward to rereading my writing and feeling accomplished as I filled the pages. When stuck for ideas, I took my daybooks down from the shelf and leafed through them, often chuckling at my doodlings. What I was thinking had a permanent home in a daybook. As the daybooks multiplied, I began to see how much I was growing as a writer. I knew instantly that my elementary students would be able to see their growth as well.

Becoming Writers with Our Students

Karen's story is a story shared by all of us. As our classrooms became places for writing and thinking rather than filling in blanks and regurgitating information, our students became excited with us about their stories, their ideas, their learning. Because we all keep daybooks right along with our students, we are constant models and coaches for the kinds of thinking and writing we want them to do. Those of us who teach elementary school find that integrating our students' daybooks and, therefore, their thinking and writing skills across curriculums makes for better understanding and learning in all areas. Those of us teaching high school find that our students carry what they learned by using their daybooks in English courses over to other classes and disciplines. Cindy and Sally have even had many students email from universities to say that they are still using their daybooks. When Lil and Shana assign daybooks in their college classes, students have said, "I love daybooks. I kept one when I was in elementary school with Mrs. Haag or Mr. Iannone" or "Did you learn about daybooks from Mrs. U. at North Meck?" We find that the daybook is the single most powerful tool we can put into the hands of our students. Daybooks energize our teaching. Daybooks give students voice and authority. Daybooks fill our classroom with exciting ideas, with joy, and with surprise. In the next chapter we will show you how we get them started.

Introducing Daybooks to Students

When we try to do something new, we don't know what we are doing. That's the biggest challenge.

—JEFFREY KALMIKOFF

D aybooks can be difficult to explain to students—part of the difficulty is that students want to give teachers "what teachers want." When a student asks, "What do you really want us to write in this daybook?" it may sound a little weird to say, "We want you to think." In order to make daybooks work as a thinking tool, teachers need to provide some structure and they must balance that structure with ownership to make students want to use daybooks. Over the years as we have worked together with elementary children, high school and college students, and teachers, we continue to change our approaches to introducing daybooks with every new group of students as our understanding of the learning process grows.

To help introduce the daybook to our students, we bring our own to school. Students notice its bulk and messiness. We show the students how our daybook is a container, more like a kitchen drawer than a notebook. We show them our chicken-scratched notes, drafting, freewriting, prewriting, revisions, and drawings. We pass it around so our students can look closely at the stuff we've glued in, examples of good writing or ideas for writing. Karen shows students her lists, such as the one below, that help her find topics.

Some Stuff in My Daybook I Can't Live Without

labeled pictures	postcards
photos	topic ideas
letters and notes	wonderful words
cutouts from newspaper handouts	phrases
sticky notes	favorite lines
parts of stories	advice
others' stories	settings
poems	character sketches
pictures	books I've read
ticket stubs	notes
comics	

Cindy shows her students the messiness of freewriting and how one line becomes the gem mined from these pages. Lil shows her students how she copies down language—poems, phrases from the paper, bumper stickers—and reflects on the impact of those words on her life. When we work with teachers who don't have a shelf of daybooks to draw from, we invite them to start one along with their students. That way, they can show students how their daybooks are growing. They can do a minilesson about how they have included a theatre ticket or a movie ticket, for example, and some notes in their daybook.

We write badly sometimes (often), but we no longer mind showing students or teachers our false starts. Any writing helps us exercise our writing muscles privately, we explain. Showing students our daybooks, with their difficulties and breakthroughs alike, emphasizes that figuring out how to use one may not go as smoothly as they think it will. It also dispels the notion that keeping a daybook is easy for us, too. We let them tell us it's hard because we know it can be at times. Showing our daybooks also helps students and teachers understand that each page doesn't have to be perfect or filled with writing. (See the Theory Box on p. 19.) We have all kinds of things in our daybook—writing, mainly, but pictures, and doodles, and photographs as well.

We each have our own style, as do the countless teachers we have introduced to the daybook over the years. That's the beauty of this tool; it's like a great recipe in the hands of a wonderful chef, who takes the basic premise and then tweaks it to her taste and expertise.

Karen's Introduction to Daybooks: An Elementary Literacy Coach's Perspective

I begin my first writing lesson the first day of school by asking, "What if you had to make a living off the writing you do? How would you live life differently if you had to pay for your shelter, your food, your clothes, and your fun from the writing you sold each month?" At first, my students just stare at me as if I'm posing a rhetorical question. When I encourage them to talk with another student or two near them, they realize I really do want an answer.

I record their suggestions on chart paper: *write every day*, *study others' writings*, *collect good writing and tips*, and *read*! The list develops slowly at first, but then the ideas start flowing:

- find out who would buy the work;
- ask other people to read and edit the pieces;
- keep troublesome-word spelling lists;
- buy journals to write in and favorite pens and pencils;
- purchase computers, a thesaurus, and a good dictionary; and
- create a space at home to write in and find a trusted writing buddy.

After the brainstorming session, I explain the relationship between the behaviors they have just proposed and success in writing class this year. Because they put energy into creating the list, they see the relationship between their jobs as students and writers' jobs as writers. The chart stays up all year as a reminder.

Finally, I ask, "If there were a tool that helped people have fun and succeed at school, you would want to know about it, right?" My students are intrigued, and it's the perfect time to introduce the daybook, which we learn how to use throughout the year to help us be writers.

Tony's Introduction to Daybooks: A Fourth-Grade Teacher's Perspective

A few years ago, I decided not to have my fourth graders compartmentalize their thinking. I didn't want them to create walls between the subjects we were studying throughout our day. I wanted my students to make connections and see the bigger picture, to bring together ideas that they learn in social studies with the literature and science we studied. I wanted students to delve deeper into their thinking, to tear down the walls that prohibit complex thinking, to understand that brains are wired for synthesizing. I wanted to create thinking that knocks walls down, and opens up pathways to higher levels of learning. The daybook helped me get there, and it's something I introduce to my students every year.

To show my students how to capture their thinking in words on a page, I create a narrative that allows the daybook to speak to the students, so that they see themselves in conversation with their daybook. I draft the narrative through the eyes of the daybook on a half sheet of paper. Students place it on the first page of their daybook at the beginning of each marking period. I encourage students to read the narrative and respond to it, thus creating a relationship between themselves and their daybook. Here is an example of where we begin.

The Long Strange Trip Begins . . .

Hey guys, I'm so excited that you are in Mr. I.'s classroom. You are going to learn some really cool things in here. Mr. I. wants you to write down all of your thinking. Yea, that's right, all of your thinking . . . in *everything*, math, social studies, language arts. Mr. I. is really into this writing. Wait 'til he shows you the blog! He is going to ask you to write down your thoughts right here and then to use those ideas when you are blogging. I'll keep your writing for you, so you won't have to worry about it getting lost. So tell me about yourself. Who are you?

Later, during the second marking period, I continue having the daybook speak to the students:

The Long Strange Trip Continues . . .

Second Marking Period
Oh my . . . where did the first nine weeks of school go? I can't believe we're starting the second marking period today! We certainly learned a lot of new and exciting things in the first marking period. It was fun being the place where you did most of your thinking and learning and I really look forward to helping you continue the long strange trip Mr. I. calls fourth grade as we embark on a brand new marking period. What goals do you have for this marking period? What do you want to learn? Don't tell Mr. I. I'm doing this, but here's a sneak peek at what you'll be learning this marking period. . . .

Mathematics   Starting today and for the next five weeks, you'll be learning how to multiply and divide. I'm sure you know how to do this a bit right now. However, Mr. I. will be teaching you new ways to do both operations and challenging you to think about both in ways you never have before. You'll also learn about number properties and the order of operations.

Reading   Mr. I. plans on starting novel studies with you in the form of literature groups. You'll start to see how this is going to work this week. Mr. I. is really excited to get going with these. He's used information you gave him at the beginning of the year to choose novels you'll be interested in reading.

Writing   You'll continue to work with the writing process in order to discover your own process when it comes to writing. This will include a lot of freewriting followed by learning more revision strategies that make your writing look and sound more interesting. You'll also get a chance to learn how to edit your writing and publish another piece like you did in the first marking period. We'll also spend more time learning how to use the *Mindings Collage* disk [see Chapter 6: The Daybook Goes Digital] Mr. I. had you play with early in the first marking period.

Social Studies   You'll continue to work with Mr. Moran's class in Melbourne, Australia. During this time, we'll complete the team project. This will include time spent on creating a webpage that contains all of the incredible information you're learning from Mr. Moran's students. We'll also be traveling to IBM in early December to take part in a video conference with our new friends in Melbourne.

Remember . . . don't tell Mr. I. I told you all of this. Now that you have the inside scoop on what we're doing . . . let's get started! Are ya ready?

I like to consider my work with children as a never ending trip . . . a journey. The students look forward to the daybook's next narrative and enjoy responding to it. The daybook gives my students a chance to discover, think, and reflect— and to keep track of all that thinking along the way.

connection Grades 6–12

Though Karen's and Tony's activities are geared toward elementary children, they can be easily adapted to the middle school, high school, or college classroom. Karen's question about what a person would need to do if she were to make her living as a writer, depending on her words for income, may be closer to the experiences of high school and middle school students. Middle school children working on the school newspaper or literary magazine, high school students who are actively involved in community service, writing op/ed pieces for the local newspaper, or writing the senior class play, have more experiences to draw on and will have a much quicker response to this question. They may even be a little bit jaded, if their prior experiences with writing haven't been wonderful. But what they will say will be very similar to the elementary children who Karen works with—a writer needs time, tools, space, community, and ideas.

Tony's idea to have the daybook speak to his students is age appropriate for fourth graders, many of whom are trying to develop the concept of writing to an audience—the daybook becomes the audience for the child's thoughts. How does this concept work in the middle or high school classroom? In a middle school class, a teacher might want to keep the talking daybook, because children still enjoy the imaginative give and take. At the high school or college level, teachers may want to adapt the strategy similarly to what Cindy and Lil describe below.

Cindy's Story: Introducing the Daybook at the High School Level

I introduce the daybook by handing my students a list of quotes by published authors talking about the messiness of writing collected in Donald Murray's *Shoptalk* (1990).

> I didn't express confidence so much as blind faith that if you go in and work every day it will get better. Three days will go by and you will think every day is terrible. But on the fourth day, if you do go in, if you don't go into town or out in the garden, something usually will break through. (50)
> —JOAN DIDION

> It may be lousy stuff. But it is there, and I can make it better tomorrow. I have done something worthwhile with my day. (58)
> —RICHARD MARIUS

> I set myself six hundred words a day as minimum output, regardless of the weather, my state of mind or if I'm sick or well. There must be six hundred finished words—not almost right words. (54)
> —ARTHUR HAILEY

> All my life I've been frightened at the moment I sit down to write. (75)
> —GABRIEL GARCÍA MÁRQUEZ

Get black on white! (58)
—GUY DE MAUPASSANT

And I don't mind writing badly for a couple of days because I know I can fix it—and fix it again and again and again, and it will be better. (75)
—TONI MORRISON

We move through a discussion of those quotes into a piece of my own entitled "Running and Writing."

Running and Writing

I may never have the words to describe a good run. Especially the feeling when I finish and the sweat cools on my back, forehead, and arms, the fresh, cool air is still pumping through my lungs, the blood is pumping through my body, and the tired muscles quiver uncontrollably. It is a special kind of afterglow.

Then there is the mental triumph, the feeling of accomplishment that comes with pushing my body for five more minutes and then ten. The mind clears, stress dissolves, problems are solved, and the soul is at peace. Along with that comes the realization that the person who once said, "I only run when someone is chasing me" is the same person who just sailed through the neighborhood with her eighty-pound dog in tow.

It has occurred to me lately that writing and running have quite a bit in common. Both take dedication and practice, and both abilities disappear if they are not used. Running is always hard for me in the beginning. I stand at the end of my driveway, Doc, my yellow lab, wagging his tail and ready to take off like a bullet. I look up the hill and think about the three miles ahead of me. Taking a long breath, I put one foot in front of the other and I am off. About halfway up the hill, my heart starts to pound, my lungs start to burst, and my legs begin to cramp. I think, "I will never make it up this hill, much less the two-and-a-half miles left ahead of me."

The stretch of pavement ahead is the blank page that must be filled with writing. I sit before my computer screen, staring at the picture of a moose with shaggy hair on my desktop, knowing that when I click on the Word icon, a blank white screen will be staring at me. I finally drag my mouse over, double-click, and there it is. I start to type one or two words and they are truly horrible. My pulse quickens, my brain cramps, and I think, "I will never be able to write the first three lines, much less fill ten pages."

I begin to think, "OK, I'll just run (or write) until I can't possibly run one more step (or write one more word)." The pain in my legs and brain is searing and I am sure that the next step/word will be my last. I know that my husband will come home to find me lying in the street or crumbled on my desk. However, that step is not my last, nor is that word, and suddenly I'm not thinking about the pain any more. My legs and brain stop cramping. I'm running without thinking, I'm writing what I'm thinking. The miles fall away and words fill the screen. I'm flying.

Sometimes when I run, I never achieve flight. Each step is painful. By the second mile, I've had it, and I walk home disappointed and sour. I talk to myself saying, "Today, I did not have a good run. But I did run; that is something. I built a little muscle today, and that will help me tomorrow when I run again. After all, even two slow, painful miles is better than sitting on the couch watching TV."

Sometimes when I write, my words never take flight. I sit and painfully churn out several pages of what I know is pure garbage. My thoughts refuse to come together and the pain in my brain never goes away. I get very little accomplished in the time that I allotted that day for writing. I tell myself, "At least I wrote and I have built a few good ideas in the pile of pages I have created. Those can be used tomorrow when I sit down to write again."

When I finish a good run, I am exhilarated, but dog-tired. I'm sweaty and worn out, but I'm also pumped up. I can't possibly rest. When I finish a good piece of writing, my eyes are blurry from staring at it and my hair is standing up all over my head. My brain feels like a big pile of mush, but I can't rest. I am totally exhilarated. In both instances, as I bask in the afterglow I think to myself, "Now why did I dread this so much, why did I get so discouraged? I know the reward for sticking this out!" I can never answer the question. I can only vow to continue to push myself again and again. (Urbanski 2006b)

After we read it together, I show them an old daybook with a draft of this piece in it. I explain that I am in the habit of freewriting daily and one day after a good run, this is what came out. This little gem became the opening for my Master's thesis and later the beginning of the first chapter of my first published book.

I have their attention, not only because my distress with writing and running resonates with many of them, but because it actually worked for me—they are seeing their teacher as a writer.

Then I hit them with it. My number one goal for the year is for each of them to see themselves as writers. That means we will write together every day and that as the year moves forward, we will learn about writing, not for some assessment, but as people who are writers. That said, I announce that we will now freewrite for fifteen minutes. Students are invited to sit on the floor, stretch their legs out, and get comfortable. They love to lie on the radiator! I tell them that they have thirty seconds to say whatever they need to say to the person beside them and then we will begin. Pencils *must* move for fifteen minutes. If they run out of something to say, they should write that. If an odd, seemingly unconnected thought pops into their minds, they should write that too. Ready . . . set . . . go!

At the end of the fifteen minutes, after some sighing and finger flexing, I ask students to take five minutes to read through what they've written and highlight anything that is at all interesting, surprising, or that they just like, even if it's only one word. They then share these gems with a partner, asking that partner to comment on what they think. The final step is to have students begin a list of things they might write about by drawing lines under their freewriting. Most students are able to come up with at least one or two things from the freewrite, many have ten or more, and a handful have nothing. Everyone is asked to pick one of those items or something completely new to freewrite about that night at home. I remind them that this is a freewrite, so they should set the kitchen timer for fifteen minutes and just go for it. As long as their pens or fingers move for fifteen minutes, that's great. We will mine for gems the next day in class.

By the end of class the next day, students have a topic for their first piece of writing of the year and many have a working draft. They also have several other topics on reserve for the next paper. They are beginning to see the power of their daybooks.

Lil's Daybook Opener: A College Teacher's Perspective

I like to give my students their first daybook as a gift, so I'm always buying composition books when they are on sale at department stores or piled in a corner, four for a dollar, at a dollar store. I typically paste a quote on the first page. When I'm teaching first-year writing, for example, I sometimes use this quote:

> *Many teachers complain that their students can't write sentences. I complain that many of my students write sentences. Too early. Following form, forgetting meaning. Following language toward correctness. For its own sake. Sentences that are like prison sentences. They don't unleash meaning, they contain meaning, compress meaning, squeeze the meaning out of language. . . . We don't know enough about how to write badly. (39)*
> —Donald Murray, *Expect the Unexpected* (1982)

This quote opens up a conversation about how our writing class is going to be different from their prior experiences writing canned essays in prefabricated formats. I don't want to read twenty-five essays that give the same three reasons to be for or against capital punishment. I want my students to explore subjects that matter to them and to write for people who matter to them. I want my students to see our class as a way for them to express their thoughts and feelings, to explore new ideas, and to lay claim to their minds. The daybook becomes our way to do that.

The second week of class I bring in this quote for students to paste in their daybooks:

> *Effective thinking isn't neat and complete. (46)*
> —Donald Murray, *Expect the Unexpected* (1982)

We all might wish that we had a lovely piece of writing like the one Cindy uses to introduce daybooks to our students, particularly to show how she had transformed it from writing in her daybook to her Master's thesis and then to her first book. Cindy's comparison of running and writing has become a quote that many of us have used with our students, giving it to them as a gift to paste into their notebooks along with the quotes that Cindy has used. The more important point Cindy makes here is that she practices what she is asking the students to do, and she has evidence to make it vivid and true. Even if you are just starting to use daybooks, you can share something that you have written for or to your students. Students love to hear about teachers' lives, and sharing a personal anecdote might be just enough for students to open up their lives with words. It is important to write the stories that will connect with our children: The time when our Mom told us to stay at home, but we went to a friend's house anyway; the time when we didn't do our chores, and our Dad came home to discover our messy room; the day our daughter learned to ride a bike. These kinds of stories develop a trusting writing community. Sharing our stories no matter the age of our students is what connects students and their teachers to daybooks.

Lil's example of using various quotes to give students lenses for looking back at what they are doing in their daybooks can be adapted easily to younger children. A teacher might pull out her copy of *Maniac Magee* and open it to the part where Maniac meets Amanda, who is carrying a suitcase full of books to school. Amanda loves books, and so does Maniac:

> There were fiction books and nonfiction books, who-did-it books and let's be friends books and what-is-it books and how-to books and how-not-to books and just regular kid books. (Spinelli 1990, 11)

This quote can get children talking about their favorite books, what they love about them, and how they might mimic the things they love in their own writing. Also, a teacher might ask children to look at several books that they have enjoyed and make lists of what intrigues them about the writing of those books. Like Karen's opening that explores what a writer needs, this activity uses books as the models rather than depending solely on children's imaginations.

This quote serves as a reminder that I'm not expecting everybody's daybook to look exactly alike. I expect them to be messy. About this time, I tell the students why I had them purchase three different colors of sticky notes. I show them how I group ideas by different colors so that I can find them when I want to write a longer paper. Within the next few weeks, the students' daybooks have a rainbow of sticky notes organizing their thoughts for the next paper. They can locate easily their thinking about particular readings, their reflections on class discussion, and their in-class freewriting that held some promise. The work marked with sticky notes can be easily distinguished from their grocery list, their new friend's cell phone number, and reminders to themselves about things that are coming due in class.

When it's time to revise, I bring in this Murray quote:

> *Look back at the writing you have done. It's probably a failure.*
> *It doesn't work as a piece of writing, not yet. Good. It doesn't need to.*
> *We don't learn from finished, polished, completed published writing.*
> *We learn from the instructive failures of early drafts. (1982, 8)*

I ask my students to reflect on the writing that they have done. What have been their "instructive failures"? How do they see their writing changing? How do they see their thinking changing?

What to Remember About Introducing Daybooks to Students

Ultimately, teachers have to come up with their own ways of making daybooks come alive to their students. There isn't just one way to do it, so it is important that teachers let theory and principles guide their practice. We all have different ways of introducing daybooks to students, but here are the things that we share in common in introducing them:

- Teachers keep daybooks themselves and model, model, model.

- Students form relationships with their daybooks as writers.

- Daybooks are the catalyst and warehouse for everything that happens in class.

- Daybooks are reflective in nature.

- Students have ownership and authority over their daybooks.

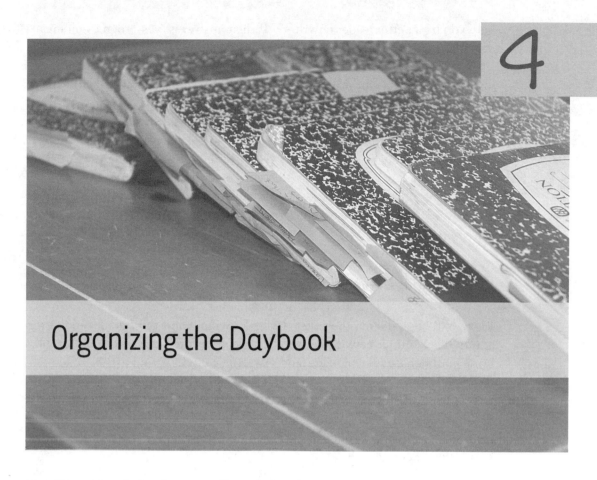

Organizing the Daybook

First things first, but not necessarily in that order.

—Dr. Who

It's hard to imagine how any one person can keep track of all that a student writes in a daybook, much less the writing of twenty-five elementary children or one hundred fifteen high school students. But through trial and error, we've figured out ways that work for us. Our secret to making daybooks an integral part of our teaching is allowing our students to make the daybook their own. By making decisions about what goes into the daybook and, as much as possible, how it is arranged, our students construct their understanding of what a daybook is *for them*.

When daybooks become part of the classroom, students will ask, "Can I put *this* in my daybook?" Our answer to that question is, "Will putting *this* in your daybook help you be a better reader or writer?" If their answer is "yes," then by all means they should write it or glue it in! After the first few days, "Will that help you be a better reader or writer?" will become a class joke. Eventually, students stop asking the question and begin shouldering the responsibility for creating their own daybook.

The number one question students and teachers ask when starting daybooks is, "How am I going to find and organize my stuff?" The beauty of the daybook is that it allows students and teachers the flexibility of discovering the structure that works for them. The six of us all organize our daybooks differently. Some of us are super organized. Others are more laissez-faire. You should use whatever seems workable from what we offer here. Mix and match, depending on your classroom.

Karen: Super Organized

I love handing children their first daybook. Second and third graders and even adults receive their new daybook with a gleam in their eye. I've seen teachers bring in ribbons, glitter, markers, and magazine pictures to add to the excitement. Some children decorate their new possession with identifying pictures, hand-writing, drawings, and add ties to keep the notebook closed when not in use.

I introduce a few must-haves in the daybook, described below, which not only encourage organization but also help me match lost notebooks to students and find pages I need to read.

▶ Table of Contents

I ask the students to leave several pages at the beginning for a table of contents and then to number the upper corners of every page in the daybook. Numbered

c o n n e c t i o n *Grades 4–12*

Organizing a daybook is related more to your personal teaching style rather than to the grade you teach. We have super-organized elementary and high school teachers mixed with a more relaxed approach across grade levels. Ultimately, it's the writer who decides how the daybook is organized. As teachers, we simply give our students ideas to choose from and models to follow until they find the method that works best for them.

pages reinforce the point that each page is important and should stay in the day-book. Students can't number all the pages in one day; neither can I. We spend a few minutes numbering and then I explain that they can finish as they have time. Keeping up with page numbering and the Table of Contents becomes part of their assigned work. On the table of contents the students write the page number and a title for each entry.

▶ Author Identification Page

Over the years, I also started requiring an author identification page. Since my day-book is so important to me, I write "Please call me if you find this daybook. I need it back!" on the very first page. I also include my name and the school phone number. A couple times that saved me—once I left my daybook at a high school and once at a meeting across town, but because a contact phone number was on the first page, I got it back. My students have turned the first page into a title page, writing who they are and how to contact them at the school. Others draw a beautiful picture on that first page. Still others write an about-the-author summary there. It's another way to make the daybook uniquely theirs. (See Figure 4–1.)

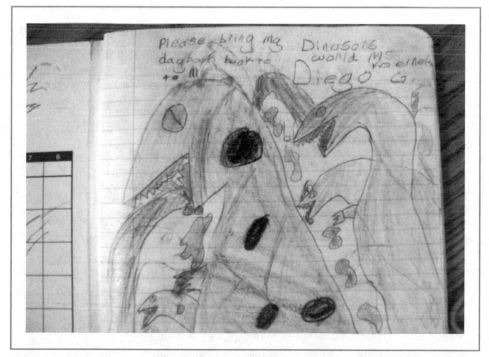

Figure 4–1 *Students elaborately decorate the author identification page; each daybook is unique to its owner.*

▶ Topic Page and Vocabulary Section

I teach my students to work from the front and the back of the daybook in order to access pages quickly. On the last page—a "one-second page," we call it, because it's a page that they can find right away—the students collect topic ideas.

Since most writers need topics, I model numerous ways to collect ideas for stories. Mem Fox (1998) challenged me to grow at the Whole Language Umbrella conference in Charlotte when she said, "I'm lucky if I find one or two topics a year! And we ask students to write on a new topic every day." So, just as kindergarteners play with punctuation until they learn how to use it correctly, my students play with finding ideas to write about.

In fact, we spend the first couple of weeks just learning how to find topics. We also set aside time to write in school. When my students know they have to write every day on a topic of their own choosing they search for ideas, think about them at other times during the day, and write ideas in their topic lists so they will always have something to write about.

From the topic page, they count back fifteen pages and make a vocabulary section, where they collect interesting words, new words, important words, and fun words. Students select words from their readings, write the page where they found the word, copy the sentence in which they found the word, write their guess of what the word means, and then look it up or ask someone. They check it if they're right or rewrite the definition in their own words. Then, every week students share the words they found in a twenty-minute vocabulary time. A pleasant surprise is how much children love collecting words. An hour can pass easily in our vocabulary time as we show and tell fun words like *onomatopoeia* and interesting words like *plant*, as in "She planted the idea in my head."

The Daybook: Making Word Learning a Natural Process

Using a daybook to teach vocabulary rather than having teacher-directed vocabulary lists allows students to discover the beauty and power of language through reading and writing. Finding words that they don't yet know in their reading or collecting fun words to use in their writing gives students opportunities to make word study a natural part of language development rather than a teacher-imposed set of requirements. When language learning is a part of writing and reading, learning new words isn't drudgery; they become an active part of students' vocabulary rather than something to be memorized one week and forgotten the next. In *Words, Words, Words*, Janet Allen (1999) offers many interesting ways to integrate vocabulary instruction into the teaching of reading and writing. Remember these ideas when you read Sally's word study in the creative writing section.

▶ Golden Lines Section

We count back another five pages from the vocabulary section and make a golden lines section. In the UNC Charlotte Writing Project, I learned about golden lines from Bob Tierney, a high school science teacher from California. He and a fourth-grade teacher friend viewed golden lines as those phrases or sentences in stories that we just must collect. When students record golden lines, they read as authors; when they discover distinctive words and phrases, they stop to savor the language. As teachers, we can model collecting golden lines for our students. For instance, I was reading a fourth-grader's paper that began, "I'm not telling this story the way it happened. I'm telling it the way I remember it." I copied that wonderful lead into the golden line section of my own daybook as my way of enjoying it, remembering it, and trying to imitate it in my own writing. I teach children to do the same.

▶ Freewriting

We freewrite to find topics; we write down everything we can think of for three to five minutes without censoring ideas. No fair lifting the pencil—we put pen to paper the whole time! Students write lists, ramblings, and stories. Nothing is wrong. Then we reread our freewrites, circle topics, and write the ideas that come to us onto our topic lists at the back of our daybooks.

▶ Lists

We make lists of things that bug us, things we love, books we've read, people we know, and so on. The students generate stories by looking at their lists. From listening to others tell stories, we think about similar experiences, and record the ideas on our topic lists. We write our own writing territories (Atwell 1987), we list what we've already written, (such as letters, emails, and stories), and who or what we write about. From our lists we search for our fallback topic, one we feel confident writing about over and over again.

▶ Using Others' Writing as Models

We look at what other people have written, such as books, titles of books, and others' daybook stories, in hopes of springboarding off their ideas and into our own. We read poems and stories and try to imitate the structure in something that we are writing. Within a couple weeks, I've launched students into writing chapter books, nonfiction books, poetry, stories, letters to the editor, and the like.

Cindy: Moderately Organized

Like Karen, I am a recovering three-ring binder girl. When I first began using the daybook in my classroom, I had visions of having all the daybooks organized exactly the same way I organized mine. The trouble was, as we moved throughout the year and filled up our daybooks, I began the next one and I organized it differently. I realized I used different organizational methods as I wrote about different things; what worked one month was silly the next. In short, I found that my students didn't need to copy my style—they could learn to create an organizational style that worked for them. Now when I introduce the daybook, I only require that everyone in the class use the same five organizational tools (described below) for the first half of the quarter, maybe longer, depending on the students.

1. Students should write their name and my name and room number in the front cover.

Like Karen's students, mine quickly find that they have loads of valuable and irreplaceable information in their daybooks. A lost daybook is disastrous, and for that reason I keep them in my classroom for many students until they begin to beg to take them home. However, if daybooks do get left around our school, they usually end up back in my hands because of their legendary status.

2. Students should number *all* pages.

As I introduce the daybook to students, they inevitably ask questions like "What page should _____ go on?" "How many pages will this take?" or "How long is this supposed to be?" I tell them that the order goes page by page—when they fill up one page, they go to the next one. I encourage them *not* to skip pages for things that they aren't finished with and plan to come back to. They can write themselves a note at the bottom of the page directing them to where to go next. The page numbers become a road map for sorting through the jumble.

3. Students should date the beginning of each entry.

I want my students to develop writing habits and come to see themselves as writers. Adding dates to daybook entries not only helps students find information in their daybooks, but also gives students the satisfaction of flipping through a full daybook and seeing those dates pop up one after another. Dating entries is a great visual for what a daily writing habit can produce.

4. Students should create a table of contents four pages from the back.

Rather than having students record every entry in a table of contents like Karen does, I encourage them to record just the important ideas they want to access quickly, the jewels they've mined from pages and pages of bad writing, the ah-has they scribbled during a discussion, the quote or picture that inspires them to write, or the list of topics they constantly reference or add to.

5. Students should create a Proofreader's guide four pages back from the table of contents.

The Proofreader's guide is a tool I learned about from Sam Watson at UNC Charlotte. Students record the common editing mistakes they make in their published pieces. When I was a tutor in the Writing Center, I learned that most students make the same mistakes over and over again, but usually they have no more than five different types and most have fewer. The students record their trouble spots and research them to create a personalized editing tool that they can reference in the final editing stage of their writing. As the year wears on I get more and more perfectly edited papers using this method. Students either learn how not to make those errors or learn to edit more carefully to avoid having to make entries in their Proofreader's guide.

▶ Gaining Independence and Ownership

Sometime around October my students really begin to understand and value their daybooks. I know we are getting there when I begin to see pictures or drawings taped and glued to the cover. Each daybook begins to take on a personal, individual look. At this point, I begin to let go of my organizational demands. The rule becomes, "As long as you can find it when we need it, it's organized." The organization doesn't have to make sense to me—it's not my daybook. I always allow

The Daybook: Helping Students Understand the Editing Process

Teaching Grammar in Context by Constance Weaver (1996) reviews the research on how children acquire grammatical competence. The research supports the teaching of grammar in the context of teaching writing rather than in isolation. Cindy's use of the daybook in the teaching of grammar gives her students a place to keep track of their own editing concerns and thereby gives them an understanding of what their particular grammatical pitfalls are. When students return to their writing, they can edit for their own individualized issues rather than concern themselves with the thousands of grammatical rules, most of which they practice intuitively because they use and practice English.

students to open it to the page I need to see or to the page they want to show me and then direct me to where I should go from there.

Some students get tired of gluing in handouts and create pockets for these papers in the back of their daybooks. Some students use sticky notes to mark pages; some take it a step further and develop some sort of code. I write notes on my sticky notes that I can see. One student wrote only on one side of the page and then flipped the daybook upside down when he got to the end and wrote his way back to the front. The daybooks become theirs and when that happens, I don't have to worry about them getting lost anymore.

Sally's Organization for Creative Writing Class

Daybooks in my classes have no divisions. Everything is recorded on a daily basis. I do ask students to skip several pages at the beginning of their daybooks to use as a table of contents. Some students do discover that they have more entries than they have lines and pages in their table of contents section. For these students, I suggest that they type the table of contents to get more entries on the pages and then paste the typed page into the daybook. I want the students to experience the idea of mushing everything together because that's the way life is— a little of this and a little of that every day rather than a day of this and a day of that. Too often in high school, subjects come in boxes: first period we open our English box and close it for second period when we open our physics box, and so on through the day, making few if any connections among the subjects. In my years in the classroom I have discovered that students often can give me a ready definition of simile, metaphor, and so on, but are not as successful at applying that definition to work. By putting a definition page next to a page of freewriting or a page of golden lines, they often review the pages simply by going through their notebooks as they search for a specific item.

▶ Golden Lines with a Twist

For creative writing and English classes, I require my students to find golden lines in a book or an English assignment they are reading. Along with the golden line, they write a reason for the choice, using literary terms they need to know for the North Carolina ninth-grade End of Course test, the tenth-grade writing test, and just to enter the conversation of writers. Students are encouraged to analyze their choices of golden lines for two reasons: to make themselves better writers by analyzing the writing of others and using their techniques, and to become better readers by understanding the techniques that writers use to make their prose or poetry interesting and informative. On Fridays, we turn the golden line collections into a book talk seminar. We put our desks in a circle and each student shares a golden line. The students look forward to this day because they have an opportunity to talk about their own books and learn about others. Often books are passed from one student to another when a golden line piques interest. Students choose favorite authors and imitate them. One of my students studied Emily Dickinson, carefully examining her diction, meter, rhyme scheme—all the Dickinsonian characteristics—recorded them in her daybook, and then imitated Dickinson until her own style emerged, different from Dickinson, but with a faint whisper of the poet's voice behind her own. Other students have recorded conversations and dialects in their daybooks as ways of entering writing.

▶ *Word Study*

Students also are required to record new and/or interesting words they encounter in all of their reading. They look up the definition, the part of speech, and the origin of the word. Once a week we share the words, each student offering one word, and these words become somewhat of a class vocabulary list, with words and definitions copied into daybooks. Every couple of weeks, students choose a word from a list other than their own, copy it at the top of a page in their daybooks, and write a free-association piece from that word. Often the free association becomes a draft for a new piece of writing. At the very least students have worked with a new word, have some notes for a future writing session, and they have had permission to let their minds wander in any direction for a while—a precious respite from the Dickens-inspired Gradgrind-ian testing tasks they are forced to endure most of their school day. I take the students' interesting words, put them into a PowerPoint slide show, and loop the show onto the television screen. The words on the TV provide background to whatever else we are doing

connection Grades 4–12

For teachers who like Sally's idea of having students select and analyze golden lines from their reading, they should look at Karen's method for organizing golden lines. Where Sally's organization is chronological and students write golden lines on the next blank page, Karen has a special section of the daybook for students to collect their favorite lines, and this section is easy to locate.

in class and give reinforcement to learning new words to those students who can't keep their eyes off the screen.

After students get the hang of finding interesting words, they start a contest to see who can find the coolest one. One student's contribution, *sesquipedalian*, was an immediate hit. The other members of the class liked the way the word rolled off their tongues—and said it over and over. They liked the definition, "given to the use of long words." And they liked the pictures the sound of the word and/or its definition conjured in their heads. Thus was born the Sesquipedalian Club, an organization of wordmeisters and writers. Some members of the club continue to meet, daybooks in hand, at a local coffeehouse for a discussion of writing and words.

▶ *Freewriting*

All of my classes begin each day with a fifteen-minute freewrite, which students begin on the next blank page of our daybooks. Later we revisit this writing to find topics for essays, poems, and stories. I encourage students to review their freewrites weekly to find patterns, repetitions, and other signals that something needs to be written before it gets away or loses its impetus. In creative writing classes, the writing is most often totally free—students just write whatever comes to mind. In English classes, the freewrite often is focused as an exercise to recall the reading assignment or a previous class discussion, which helps students identify various parts of the author's style, relate the piece to another author or piece, or enhance the understanding of a term, as well as serve as review for future papers and tests. During freewriting, my students often paste weekly poetry responses into their daybooks as a reference as well as scan, print, and paste poems or whole passages from books that they particularly like. Their daybooks become their thinking books, ready at any time to help them recall a thought or to think out a new thought on a blank page.

Tony's Organizing Scheme: Middle of the Road

I don't get as organized as Karen and Cindy do when it comes to my daybook and what I expect from my students' daybooks. I guess I'm more like Sally. To me, the daybook should be free-flowing and the entries should happen on an organic level rather than preplanning out x number of pages for this and y number of pages for that. However, that is the beauty of daybooks—there is no correct format. Sometimes it's more fun just to let things happen.

My students and I only have a few things that are standard in terms of the organization of our daybooks. I like putting a message at the beginning of the daybook. I write this message to the students as if it were the daybook speaking to them. This message helps my young writers imagine a reader, an audience, for their daybooks. I ask my students to count out four to five pages at the back of their daybook to be used as an index. The entries in the index must have whatever heading the student gives a particular page as well as its page number. Students are able to reference pages much quicker if their index is up-to-date. It also helps out in class when I want students to look back and find their work. For example, I may ask a student to find the page where she has written a double-entry response to a novel that we read three weeks ago. Rather than paging through the entire daybook, all she has to do is go to the index and look for the appropriate heading. Other than that, the sky's the limit! I see daybooks as a tool one takes on a long strange trip—we can learn a lot from reflecting back at the end of our journeys.

Shana's Organized Chaos

I went to college on an athletic scholarship for soccer. As with any sport, our team had to do a warm up before each game. The warm-up involved a series of running and stretching exercises that we did in unison. After the warm-up, we moved into our individual time, and this is where I really got ready for the game. We split up according to our positions and did whatever we felt necessary to physically and mentally prepare for the game. Some would sit and stretch while others would race around the field with the ball, and still others would pass the ball to each other among everyone else. Now to anyone watching this phase of our game preparation, it would look like mass chaos because very few players were doing the same thing. Yet, in the end, we all wound up ready for kickoff. We just had different but equally effective ways of arriving at that point. I use this experience to teach students how to organize their daybooks.

Just as my teammates and I had to do our own thing to prepare for each game, I feel it is important for my students to have the freedom to organize their daybooks in a way that helps them prepare for the game of reading and writing. When students first choose their daybooks, I recommend my students buy the tried-and-true composition notebook. However, I do allow them the freedom to purchase any equally sturdy, composition-size journal they desire. My students grow very attached to these containers of thought, and I want them to appreciate not only what is on the inside pages of the daybook but also how it looks on the outside. If a journal with a picture of a daisy on the cover makes one of my students appreciate and grow more fond of her daybook, then I encourage her to buy it.

When it comes to organizing daybook pages, I do not require any formal table of contents, but I do ask my students to date each new class period and the entries for that day as well as number their pages. This minimal record keeping helps students keep track of assignments, which I always prepare daybook size (landscape and cut in half). They can find their prewriting for an assignment the class started on a certain day or quickly see what page numbers need to be copied for the daybook section of their final portfolios. I typically do not collect daybooks, but rather ask students to select pieces from their daybooks that illustrate certain types of learning throughout the semester. (See Chapter 7 on assessment.) The most important aspect for me, as the teacher, is to let my students discover what works for them in regards to the organization, which is also how we approach our writing.

The Ultimate Organizational Invention: Landscape Handouts

A really cool organizing idea we all use is the landscape handout. We create these handouts in one of two ways. One way is to create a one-page handout as one normally would in portrait view on 8-1/2-by-11-inch paper. Then copy page one onto page two. When it is time to print, select *pages per sheet* on the Word print menu and then select the two-pages-per-page option. (If Word remains one of those weird mysteries of life, look on the right hand side of the print menu, just under the *number of copies* option. There is an area called *zoom*. Here is where you select *pages per sheet*.) Word then prints out the handout in landscape mode with two copies of the handout per page.

The second way to create the handouts is to select *landscape* in the *page setup* option located under the file menu. We have found it easier once the page is in landscape to set up the document as two columns. In column one, type the contents for the handout. Then copy the handout to the second column. Word does strange things when you work in columns—it changes numbers mysteriously, and we all have found ourselves making up funny excuses when students ask, "Where are numbers one through four? My handout has five through eight only." Therefore, we double-check our work before printing, but essentially we select the normal print options (unlike the first scenario above) and wind up again with two copies of the handout per page.

Once we create the handouts, we cut the pages in half. The resulting page glues easily into the daybook without creating too much bulk. Since teachers get two handouts to a page they cut their copying costs in half, which is an important aspect in most schools.

What to Do When You Finish a Daybook

Just as each of us organizes our daybooks differently, we each have a different way of organizing them once we have completed one and started another. Each of us has many daybooks lined up on our shelves. Some of us label our daybooks by using a silver permanent marker to write on the black spine. Others remember each daybook by how we have decorated the cover. Still others write in black ink the time period that the daybook covers on a white label, and stick the label on the spine of the daybook. Most of us arrange our daybooks chronologically on the shelf, which shows the order of our thinking and writing.

What to Remember About Organizing Daybooks

No matter where you are on the organizational continuum from super organized to organized chaos, the main thing to remember is that the students' writing is what matters. You, along with your students, will discover ways to manage the daybooks and to find the gems of writing that make all the exploration valuable.

- Teachers model, model, model.

- Students need to make their daybooks their own, so be flexible. Just two important principles for students:
  - Students are in total control of their daybooks.
  - Students must always be able to find their work when they need it.

- Everybody invents new ways of finding material in their daybooks. Share those strategies.

- When entries are dated and pages are numbered, material is easier to find.

- Names and contact information should be somewhere in daybooks, so that if they are forgotten in the cafeteria or left on the school bus, they can be returned to the writer.

- Label daybooks by using a silver permanent marker to write on the black spine or sticking a white label with a title on the spine.

Sustaining Daybooks
Creating the Toolbox

Few things are impossible to diligence and skill. Great works are performed not by strength but perseverance.

—Samuel Johnson

Once daybooks get started, one of two things can happen. They either take on a life of their own or they get lost in the maze of school activities. To keep daybooks an active part of a classroom means that teachers should use them as part of daily thinking and learning. Helping students to sustain their daybooks means that teachers constantly give students new tools to use. As more tools become available, students develop a toolbox, a repertoire of strategies that work for them when writing for different purposes or audiences.

Karen's Daybook Tools:
An Elementary Literacy Coach's Perspective

Even if I only find ten minutes to write a couple times a week in my daybook, I never fail to find lesson ideas in it. It beats buying expensive writing programs, leafing through so-called writing books, or assigning workbook pages I have to patrol to get kids to do.

Every story I write has several minilessons embedded within it: How I got my idea, how I broke through my stuck points, my revision, the ideas I kept for another time, and the editing errors my husband found that I didn't. Through daybook minilessons, my students and I bond over writing struggles, such as wrestling with blank pages and lamenting the lack of time to write. Our daybooks are where my students practice and hone the strategies they learn in these minilessons; the strategies then become the tools they use as writers.

I teach minilessons on how to give responses to writers' drafts, for example, showing students how to take notes in their daybooks while writers read their stories. Responses are grouped by compliments, questions, and suggestions. All the students have responses because they all have taken notes. Over time they can look back on their earlier responses to notice ways they have grown or changed as responders.

I teach minilessons on several revision strategies, such as adding detail to the story, developing exciting openings, and changing story line to dialogue. Students apply the revision strategies from the minilesson to early ideas they have been working on in their daybooks. Because they do this early writing and revision in their daybooks, students realize that their writing is not chiseled in stone but is part of the drafting process. Students often discover that play with language can produce ideas that become part of a draft that they want to work on further. When they are ready to draft further, they move their work outside of the daybook onto notebook paper or to the computer.

▶ Using Double-Entry Journals Across the Curriculum

We're not always aware what our brains are thinking. We often take our thinking for granted. To counteract that problem, I teach students to record their thinking in their daybooks. One process that slows them down enough to be metacognitive is writing in two-column notes, or double-entry journals, in their daybooks. They fold a daybook page in half the long way so that two columns are readily accessible.

I then give them a strategy for keeping track of unfamiliar words by putting two headings at the top, *new word* on the left and *how I figured it out* on the right. For example, on the left side a child could write the tough word with which she had struggled and on the right side she could write all the reading strategies she knew and used. She then would learn that sometimes she may need more than one strategy.

Another double-entry strategy I give them to use when they are reading is to put *confusing part* on the left and *the connection that helped me get unconfused* on the right side of the daybook page. The columns change depending on what we study. *What I observe* and *what I wonder* is a favorite double-entry choice for many young readers and writers. When we study the tools authors use to help readers understand what's going on in a story, we explore *clues I noticed* and *literary element I will share*. When reading nonfiction, students can quote specifics from the text on the left and what concept of print they found on the right side of the page.

Daybook Double-Entry Journal Options

- unfamiliar words: new word/how I figured it out

- connections: confusing part/how I got unconfused

- questioning: notice/wonder

- author study: clues/literary element

- social studies (nonfiction): fact/opinion or notice/concept of print (bold, italic, and so on)

▶ *Partner Journals*

Another popular activity for the daybook toolbox is partner journaling. One student can write to a partner either to address an open-ended question such as, "What reaction did you have to the chapter today?" or they may write to address a more specific task such as: "Tell your partner what you learned about reading today and how you plan to use your new learning." The pair exchanges daybooks and writes back in a letter form. Students often write themselves into an understanding of a text. Often a partner can clear up a confusing point by writing back. Also, the activity takes pressure off the teacher to read and respond to every daybook.

▶ The Reading/Writing Connection

Double-entry journals and partner journals are all part of the daybook preparation students are expected to do before they come to a literature circle or book discussion. Their daybook writing beforehand makes the discussion lively and engaging. I watch children argue their theories, pointing to evidence in texts with their daybooks and their novels spread out on the table. I see engagement in their faces as they struggle with difficult questions. Often hand goes to chin, eyes widen, and children leaf through their daybooks as they puzzle out answers to difficult questions they posed in the first place. Students store their questions that hit them as they're reading in their daybooks; their ideas are not lost.

Sometimes, students rely on book discussions solely to help them clarify what they don't understand. However, I ask my children to look for the treasures embedded in the texts that others might miss, like foreshadowing clues and metaphors. They bring questions to get help from their classmates. Eventually, students tackle more difficult thinking tasks. I teach them to read as detectives and to bring to their literature circles their ideas about what might signal an author's purpose or theme. Helping each other explore a novel improves everyone's comprehension.

▶ Dealing with the Tests

Students used to thinking in their daybooks breeze through statewide reading comprehension tests or statewide writing tests. In North Carolina, our third graders take a reading comprehension test and in fourth grade they take a statewide writing test, which is a narrative. Teachers often ask me how students can make the transfer from selecting writing topics on their own and having opportunities to revise their work to test-taking demands like writing to a prompt and writing in timed situations. My experience shows me that children must write about what they know in order to gain confidence in their abilities. Students can't be struggling with content and writing skills at the same time. I find it much easier to teach them the skills after they find the joy. Some ways I help students find their own narrative topics include:

- freewriting to discover what you're thinking about

- reading book titles and books to get ideas

- making lists, such as "A List of Things That Bug Me"

- brainstorming—dumping all that's on your mind onto the paper in list form

- sharing stories to generate story ideas

- listening to what's going on around you

- determining what you know a lot about—finding your expert topic

- talking to others

- remembering when . . .

- retelling stories from television, movies, or books from another's perspective

I let students choose their own topics as much as possible to help them get their writing legs. Then we continue writing in our daybooks, choosing the tools we need to solve various writing problems and help our writing grow. When test day nears and we finally get around to talking about the test, my students say, "This test is no big deal, we're writers." My principal told me that she had never seen our fourth graders have such confidence about our writing test. They came to school with smiles on their faces, pencils at the ready, bursting with pride to show the state what they knew about writing. Once children have written their own stories, they can relate their ideas to the test prompt and draw on their tool-box of writing strategies.

c o n n e c t i o n Grades 6–12

Middle school and high school students in our state and across the country are asked to take standardized writing assessments along with other tests such as the SAT, a myriad of reading comprehension tests, and subject area assessments. If we only ask students to write to prompts *or* if we only ask students to write what they know, they fail our state tests. Either way they do not do well. All of our students, just like Karen's, need to have the test demystified. But that is the last step, not the first step. Writing and becoming a writer come first. Then as the test date approaches, writers already know what they need to know. Becoming a writer and feeling the joy of writing is how we spend 99 percent of our time. Only 1 percent of our time is spent on the test—and in that time, we are showing them that they already know everything they need to know. As for the other tests, just as with the writing assessments, if we focus on teaching students to think critically about the subject areas already in their daybooks, the tests take care of themselves.

Cindy's Daybook Tools:
A High School English Teacher's Perspective

Karen introduced the daybook to me and that is quite evident in my classroom. I use everything she's discussed so far. That said, I'd like to add three more tools to the toolbox: quickwrites, dialectic response journals, and multigenre responses.

▌ Quickwrites

Linda Rief (2003) coined the phrase *quickwrites*. In my mind a quickwrite is a focused freewriting, where students write nonstop for three minutes on the topic at hand. I sometimes use the quickwrite several times in a class period, especially when we are discussing a complex topic in literature. When the discussion gets heated, or if there seems to be a lull, I ask students to write for a few minutes in their daybooks about their thoughts on the subject. It's quick, it's easy, and it's simple.

▌ Dialectic Response Journals

The dialectic response journal is a great way to begin conversation and discussion, especially in, but not limited to, those classes that stare silently at their teacher when asked what they think. This tool also works well with really chatty classes because it allows and encourages students to write notes to each other. It combines Karen's description of the daybook double-entry journal with a partner journal and adds two more columns. The note-taking and note-making portions are in the first and second columns; a third column is added for the journal partner to respond; the fourth column is for the writer's synthesis of and reflection on the first three columns.

Daybook Dialectic Response Journal

1. Create four columns in your daybook.

2. Reserve column one for note taking.
   - quote
   - summary
   - question about the text

3. Reserve column two for your response to column one.
   - Think about the significance.
   - Think about the author's purpose.
   - That is causing you to have this question about the text?

4. Reserve column three for a response from another person.
   - agree/disagree
   - extend
   - question

5. Reserve column four for "What I'm Thinking Now."
   - ideas solidified
   - new questions raised
   - questions answered
   - new ideas

Students often complete the first two columns at home and then we use the beginning of the class period to swap daybooks with and write to each other. Sometimes we go directly into large or small group discussions from there, and other times we work on the fourth column before moving on, depending on the day and the needs of the students.

▶ Multigenre Response

In *Blending Genre, Altering Style: Writing Multigenre Papers* (2000), Tom Romano shows readers the kind of thinking students can do if they are allowed to and encouraged to think through different genres on a topic. Romano's book piqued my interest because he has students write entire crafted pieces in multigenre style. I adapted his idea for the daybook and call it the *multigenre response*. The following is the multigenre response assignment I present to my students at the start of the year.

The beauty of multigenre response for me is captured in the first line of the quote in the assignment from Tom Romano, "Genres of narrative thinking require writers to be concrete and precise." Students can't hide behind abstract, regurgitated language. They must delve into the idea for an opinion or view about it and then represent that in a concrete way that others can comprehend. When we finish our forty-five minutes of writing and pull our desks into a circle to share, students who were typically reluctant to share writing or even speak during discussion are hopping in their seats. We laugh together, we cry a little, and over and over we say, "Oh, I hadn't thought about it that way!" to students who have never before elicited that response.

MULTIGENRE RESPONSE

What Is It?

A multigenre response is responding to literature through a variety of narrative genres rather than through expository abstract language.

Why Multigenre?

"Genres of narrative thinking require writers to be concrete and precise. They can't just tell in abstract language. They can't just be paradigmatic. They must show. They must make their topics palpable. They must penetrate" (Romano 2000, 26). Using a multigenre approach forces the writer to "consider the nature of and the emotions behind the material [he or she] is reporting" (Romano 2000, 26).

Your Mission

1. Pick a character from your reading assignment. Major characters are certainly acceptable, but one of the minor characters may be more interesting. Jot down a few notes about that character. Think about physical appearance, life philosophy, social position, and personality. Go to the book and find some textual support for the analysis of that character.

2. Choose one of the following to try to *show* us this character

   - a free-verse poem
   - a poem in the character's voice
   - a monologue
   - a newspaper article
   - a want ad
   - a résumé
   - a collection of recipes
   - a poem in two voices
   - a dialogue between the two consciousnesses of the character
   - a CD song list
   - a recipe book
   - a comic strip
   - a political cartoon
   - a genre of your choice

   You have forty-five minutes to create a draft. Go for it. Experiment! Have fun! We will share some of these in class.

The bottom line for me is that the multigenre response taps into students' strengths and their imaginations. The rocker can do his CD list; the jock can do *Sports' Illustrated* analysis; and the girls in black can do their Animé. The multigenre response gives them a chance to play again with literature and writing, and in that seeming play do some powerful thinking that can later be incorporated into a literature essay. Writing in their daybook frees them from having to focus on technical competence, evaluation, and academic alienation, and lets them think without the constraints that teachers often impose on writers.

A Daybook Tool from Tony: Adaptation of Smagorinsky's Body Biography

A great activity to get students thinking about literature is the body biography, which Peter Smagorinsky (2001) observed a teacher doing with her high school students. I knew immediately that it could be adapted for my elementary students. (See Figure 5–1.)

Teachers can use Smagorinsky's body biography instructions (2001) as written or adapt them to the abilities of their students. For instance, an elementary teacher may want to introduce one idea at a time, such as having students draw an outline of the body and then write different lines from the story that they think are significant. Middle and high school teachers may be able to use the instructions as they are written.

As my students reach the midway point of their current novel study, I ask them to join me on the carpet for a discussion. I tell my students that they will become literary critics by learning a new way to respond to their reading through drawing and writing what is called a body biography. This introduction naturally peaks their curiosity. I start by handing them a copy of the body biography guidelines, though we work through the guidelines slowly so that I am sure that each child understands what we are doing.

connection Grades 4–6

Karen and Cindy use many of the same toolbox strategies. Cindy has added a few more, but these can be easily adapted for elementary students. All students can connect with their reading through multigenre response or through talking with a partner on paper about their differing responses. All of us could use the time to think in the midst of learning new ideas offered by the quickwrite. The only real difference is the speed at which students become independent in choosing the most appropriate tool from the toolboxes they have created for the concepts that they are working with.

Body Biography

PURPOSE

This is a creative way to discuss a character in the literature you're reading.

INSTRUCTIONS

For your chosen character, create a body biography—a visual and written portrait illustrating several aspects of the character's life within the story.

You have many possibilities for filling up your sheet of paper. The choices you make should be based on the text. You will be verbally explaining (in your discussion group) the choices you made while you show your classmates your finished product. Make sure your choices are creative, show that you've been thinking, and are accurate.

Here are some hints as to what your classmates should see and feel as a result of your sharing:

- Review important events, choices, and changes involving your character.
- Communicate the full essence (heart) of your character, emphasizing the traits that make her or him who she or he is.
- Get your classmates talking about your character.

BODY BIOGRAPHY REQUIREMENTS

Although it should contain other things—remember to be creative—your body biography should include:

- a review of important events in the story;
- visual symbols;
- original text; and
- at least two sentences from the novel that clearly represent your character.

BODY BIOGRAPHY SUGGESTIONS

1. **Placement:** Carefully choose the placement of your text and artwork. For example, the area where your character's heart would be might be appropriate for illustrating the important relationships within your character's life.

2. **Spine:** What is your character's objective (what does she or he want to accomplish) in the story? What is her or his goal? What drives her or him? Are there interesting ways to illustrate this?

3. **Virtues and Vices:** What is your character's most admirable quality? Worst? How can you make us visualize him or her?

4. **Color:** Colors are often symbolic. What colors do you most associate with your character? Why? How can you work these colors into your illustration?

(continued)

Figure 5–1 *Peter Smagorinsky's body biography (2001) instructions.*

5. **Symbols:** What objects can you associate with your character that illustrate her or his essence (heart)? Are there objects within the story you could use? If not, choose some that you think relate to your character.

6. **Acrostic poem:** This is a fast and effective way to produce text that will reveal a lot about a character.

7. **Mirror, Mirror:** How does your character appear to others in the story versus what you know about the character's inner self? Do these images clash or go together?

8. **Changes:** How has your character changed over the course of the story? Trace these changes (steps) within your text and/or artwork.

Figure 5–1 (*continued*)

I ask students to begin by drawing in their daybooks the outline for the body of the character they want to describe. I tell them that they need to include four things, though they are free to use others as well:

- a review of important events in the story;
- visual symbols;
- original text; and
- at least two sentences from the novel that clearly represent the character.

If the student follows these guidelines, she has reviewed the story and begun to analyze the literature from her own vantage point. She has a visual representation of her thinking to take to her group to begin discussion. To prepare students to share their drawings and writings in their literature groups, I ask them to be sure that they have:

- communicated the full essence (heart) of the character emphasizing the traits that make her or him who she or he is; and
- represented their character in such a way that will get their peers interested.

Gloria chose to represent Houdini in her body biography after reading the biography *Harry Houdini* (Cobb 2005), and she did a great job of integrating ideas. She drew Houdini getting punched by someone, which, as legend has it, caused the appendicitis that led to Houdini's death. The text she pulled from the book, "Is it true that you can take a blow to the stomach without any pain?" (120) relates to the drawing, and she has included a picture of an x-ray of Houdini's appendix as her symbol. The phrase "10 Days Later . . ." made a great transition that highlighted the student's before and after perspective of the event she was writing and drawing about. She drew Houdini's wife, Bess, and others who knew and loved Houdini at the bottom of the picture, and it was no accident that they are surrounding the words from the book. Looking at Gloria's original text—(in this case a summary of the events that she's drawn)—I can see that she's worked very deliberately to make sure that there is a thread of consistency in every aspect of the body biography. (See Figure 5–2.) I get the impression that she tuned in to Houdini as a person and the events that centered on his death.

Figure 5–2   *Gloria's body biography of Houdini shows her complete knowledge of the subject.*

Gloria's body biography shows a high level of comprehension of the book she has read and discussed with her classmates. As a result she has given us an interesting analysis of the literature in a creative way. Her work tells me a lot more about her knowledge than any multiple choice test ever would.

Lil's Daybook Tools for Reading Complex Texts

Daybooks are a great way to engage students in reading complex texts, either literary texts or argumentative and theoretical texts. I have students focus their readings and write about their ideas in their daybooks using various tools.

▌*Mapping the Text*

Mapping a text is a great tool to use when students are struggling with complicated readings. I begin by having students create their own maps in their daybooks after they have read a particularly hard essay. In small groups in class, I ask them to share their maps and then develop one map for their group that gives their best reading of the essay. The maps the students create often amaze me. (See Figure 5–3, p. 56.) Rather than me having to explain every difficult concept in the essay, the students are able to work collaboratively to think critically about and understand the text. An example of how I introduce text maps to my students is on the following page.

▌*Keeping Track of Responses to Literature*

Another tool that I give my students to paste in their daybooks gives them a visual guide for keeping track of their reading of a novel, whether we are reading the novel as a class or whether the students have self-selected their novels around a theme. I ask them to record in their daybooks important words or images and the scenes from the book in which they find them. I also ask them to write down the page numbers for memorable passages or where they note shifts in meaning, tone, or point of view. The daybook becomes a way for them to keep track of their readings.

When students come to class, I ask them to freewrite on a key word, and after three minutes, I ask them to shift their focus to a key image and write for three minutes about that image. We begin class discussion with their observations. If students have selected similar words the discussion grows deeper. If students select different words, we look closely at those words to see why there are differences and how our readings give us clues to our frameworks of interpretation. (See Figure 5–4, p. 57.)

MAPPING AN ESSAY

You are to create a visual map of the essay. Your map should:

1. Designate symbolically the key parts of the essay, being sure that you cover the argument from beginning to end.
2. Introduce the road signs of the essay by indicating portions of the essay where you would want your traveler to dwell and places where the reader should stop and spend time.
3. Place scenic emblems from the essay; items from the article that the reader should consider as important to her understanding of the essay.
4. Interweave significant language from the essay within the map.
5. Introduce *symbolically* the central terms of the essay.
6. Have at least one piece of original text from the essay.

Your map should leave the viewer with a clear sense of the article and the desire to read it. You should also leave your reader with:

1. a sense of direction
2. a question to consider

The Daybook: Enhancing the Social Nature of Reading

The reading workshop that Lil describes differs from the one that Nancie Atwell talks about in *In the Middle* (1987). Atwell's workshop invites students to read self-selected novels and keep a reader's notebook about their responses to those novels. Students write reviews for their classmates who may read the novel at another time. What is missing in this kind of workshop is the excitement of sharing responses to novels and questioning ideas the way we might in a book club or a literature circle (Daniels 2002). In literature circles students can read the same book or can select books that center on a particular theme (for example, the idea of family). The theme gives the students a way of sharing their novels and their responses in small groups or to the entire class. Responses to literature begin with the reader's transaction with the text, where the text is brought into being by the ways the words of text shape and illuminate the reader's imagination. Louise Rosenblatt (1978) calls such a reading a *transaction*, where the text shapes the reader and the reader shapes the text. Rosenblatt's view of the reader gives readers agency to gather meaning from their experiences but also places the reader in history where readers are shaped by their encounters with texts. Sharing books with others using daybooks dramatizes the social nature of reading.

Figure 5—3 *Student text maps show collaboration and understanding.*

▶ *Responses to Characters and Conflict in Literary Texts*

To continue sharpening my students' focus as they read, again whether the whole group is reading the same shared novel or students are reading self-selected novels focused around a particular theme, I give them a handout that invites them to explore the importance of the characters, the setting, the conflict, and the resolution. (See Figure 5–5, p. 58.) Students glue the handout on a left-hand page in their daybooks, and they write their responses to the questions on the opposing page. The daybook tool works much like a graphic organizer, giving students a visual reminder of the ways their responses shape the text and their readings are shaped by texts. Their writing from the handout is shared during small groups. Before we begin full class discussion, I ask the students to add to their initial thinking in their daybooks what they've learned from talking with their peers.

Most important word: Image: Scene (include page number):	Shifts in meaning, imagery, tone, plot, narrator, or point of view:
Memorable passages:	Your view of main character's motives:

Figure 5—4 *A diagram to help students keep track of their literature responses.*

© 2008 by Lil Brannon et al. *from* Thinking Out Loud on Paper. *Portsmouth, NH: Heinemann.*

Character(s) important to our understanding of the novel

Name:

Internal Conflict	External Conflict

Name:

Internal Conflict	External Conflict

Setting
What is significant about where the action is happening?

What is significant about the time in which the novel takes place?

What is socially (gender, race, social class) significant and why?

What is culturally (the larger culture of which this group is part) significant and why?

Problem/Conflict
Who has power? Who wants it? Does that change within the novel?

What is significant about the central relationship(s)?

What values are at stake?

What/who is good? What/who is evil?

Who wins?

Who loses?

Resolution
What do we know at the end that we didn't know before reading the novel?

Figure 5–5 *A diagram to help students explore literary characters and conflicts.*

© 2008 by Lil Brannon et al. from Thinking Out Loud on Paper. Portsmouth, NH: Heinemann.

Sally's Daybook Tool to Eliminate Writer's Block: Metawriting

After I experienced a writer's block of mammoth proportions in graduate school, I added another dimension to the daybooks in my classes: reflection about every piece of writing that is turned in. Metawriting, writing about one's writing, increases our awareness of how we write and how we decide what we will write. It can be an invaluable tool for learning to write in a new genre or style or just spiffing up one in which we already work.

As the expectations in my classes increased, my writer's block reached a degree of total dysfunction that made me unable to write any words on the computer screen. Over and over I would write my name, the date, and the name of the class in the header. I would alter the page numbering system, save the pages, and come back later only to alter the page numbering system again. Eventually, I would get words on the pages, print them out, rewrite, print out, and so forth, but never anything I thought had the academic voice necessary for the final draft. The incompletes began to pile up as I put off the inevitable—producing a final copy and handing it in. One of my professors suggested that I keep a special daybook exclusively for writing about my writing. The requirement was that I would work on a paper every day, and when I finished writing, I would write about my writing: how I decided what to write, how I chose the words I wrote, what I thought about the finished product, how I thought I could improve.

Each page was dated, printed, and pasted into the special daybook, which grew fat in a short space of time. With the starting of my dissertation looming even closer, I had to get the writer's block behind me. At the end of each week, I read all the entries and looked for patterns. In July I wrote, "Keep searching for sources to be sure I've got it right. Can't let go. Mike Rose's essay 'Rigid Rules, Inflexible Plans, and the Stifling of Language: A Cognitivist Analysis of Writer's Block' [1980] seems to lay out some of my basic problems, but not enough to get past them. I don't have self confidence, and I worry that I will look stupid. I think everybody in the class can write better than I can, even though I see holes and mess in their writing."

Later in July I wrote, "Maybe I have found the answer. Sometimes I just have to write until I know what I am writing about and sometimes it takes a long time for me to know what I am talking about."

By December I was working against a clock, writing for long hours every day and hopeful that my problem was solved. I wrote, "I think I have found a chunk of my own writing problems. I have been reading Tom Romano's *Crafting Authentic Voice* [2004] and I can now list some of my problems." I listed the reasons I believed my writing interrupted itself and what I would change, ending with,

"This is not a New Year's resolution." The recurring phrase in all the writing was *self-confidence*. I just needed to write and to believe in myself. Two years later, in January, I wrote, "I am in some kind of euphoria from the sheer joy of writing the paper. I know what it is. I have to write the narrative. I once said 'sketch out what I think,' but it is more than that. I have to just tell a story first."

Finally it was there: I have to write in my conversational style until I've told the whole thing, then convert to academic style. Once I understood what my problem was, I stopped beating myself up. Now I just allow extra time for each piece because I've learned I have to write what I think I know before I can write.

The epiphany from my own tribulations led me to think about the students who come to my desk year after year with the same pleas: "Tell me what to write about" or "I don't know how to start this paper." Sometimes I would make suggestions and sometimes I would tell them to just sit and think for a while and it would come to them. But my experiences let me know that these students were serious in their misgivings about their own writing. They weren't killing time or trying to get me to write their papers. They truly had a block and the writing was not flowing as they had been led to believe it would. The pump needed priming—some serious reflection.

Before I started my special daybook, I asked students to include with their papers a reflection page that told me what they wanted me to look for in their work. Now I ask them to write about the difficulties and triumphs they experienced in writing the pieces. A reflection of this sort accompanies each piece and is pasted into the daybook when the paper is returned. Now complaints about writer's block are referred to their daybooks. "Write what you are having trouble with," I tell them. "Then look back and see how you handled it before or write about how you think you can handle it this time. The reflection pieces become writing manuals of sorts as the students work with problems such as thesis statements, summary of another's work, transitions, staying on topic, voice. Coupled with their freewrites and snippets of golden lines, their daybooks become invaluable sources for inspiration and writing detail.

The end of each marking period is another time for reflection and self-assessment. In their daybooks, students compile a list of all the reading they have done during the marking period and the amount of time they spent reading each item. *All reading* means just that—everything from newspapers to textbooks. Then they are to list all the writing they have done and assess the quality of the pieces: Better than last time? Not as good? Why or why not? This is to be done in essay form in their daybooks as a further reflection. Often, when they record what they have read and begin writing about their writing, they see connections between the reading and the writing. No matter how many times I tell them that reading is writing because writing reflects reading, it is at the point of their own discovery that reading plays an important part in their writing that they begin to read with more fervor.

What to Remember About Sustaining Daybooks

Daybooks make visible students' thinking and learning. Sustaining daybooks is simply a matter of showing students that they are thinkers and giving them a place to store their thinking and learning. The daybook is this place. The tools we offer in this chapter are a starting point.

- Teachers should keep a daybook along with the students and model, model, model.

- Make daybook writing an integral part of every class. Begin class by writing a few minutes in the daybook. This writing will focus the students and remind them of how important their thinking is in the classroom.

- Have students use daybooks to record their thoughts about what they are reading, experiencing, remembering, and wondering about.

- Have students look back over the writing they have done in their daybooks for patterns of their thinking, for ideas to write about, and for understanding who they are and what they think.

The Daybook Goes Digital

If we teach today's students as we taught yesterday's, we rob them of tomorrow.

—John Dewey

We realize that our daybooks are high-tech in a low-tech sort of way. But while all of us love our pen-and-paper daybooks, we realize that our students have electronic lifestyles and will someday enter a highly technological job market. They chat with each other through instant messaging while doing their homework at midnight. They have their own personal blogs where they write their diaries and explore all the angst and pleasure of growing up. At the middle and high school levels, we've noticed students regularly sending their papers to one another for comments and getting in chat rooms to discuss their reading. We see printed evidence of this in the draft work we collect. Students also send multiple drafts to us through email. The skills our students are developing with all of these experiences will serve them well as adults. Because we realize the importance of bringing all of that wonderful experimentation and learning into our classrooms rather than segregating it to our students' personal lives, several of us have experimented with more recent technologies.

The Daybook: A Bridge to Digital Literacy

Why Bother with Digital Literacy?

The difficulties associated with gaining access to technology in our classrooms are familiar for all teachers. Slogging through mud to bring a computer cart to a trailer, jockeying for position in the computer lab, cries of "mine's broken!" from frustrated students, and LCD projectors that suddenly decide they are not going to speak with the laptop all seem like valid reasons for sticking to paper and pencil. To many, the time wasted dealing with these issues could be better spent writing, talking about writing, reading students' writing, and planning lessons that help students enjoy language. However, knowing some of the theoretical underpinnings behind digital literacy will help us better understand why making use of available technologies has great potential for our students.

What we are essentially discussing in this chapter is digital literacy, often referred to as *multiliteracy* or *multimodality*. The characteristics of digital literacy embody the notion that the idea of *text* no longer merely means black type on a white page. Therefore, schools should explore, analyze, create, and learn various modes of text, essentially preparing students to be literate in their increasingly digital and multimodal world. Unlike traditional academic literacy, which is often stagnant and requires students to become literate by learning a set of skills, multimodality posits that "meanings are made, distributed, received, interpreted, and remade in interpretation through many representational and communicative modes—not just language" (Jewitt and Kress 2003, 1). Additionally, technology now plays an important role in literacy, and what is deemed as text is continually changing due to the multimodality of literacy (Selfe 1999).

Nowadays, students are often skilled in mediums other than writing. This stems from the increasing technologies produced for mass consumption in our society. Therefore, digital literacy connects the classroom to the pressures of the economy and workforce to hire technologically skilled workers; thus, schools should work to ensure that students are digitally literate. Building from these characteristics of digital literacy, as well as multimodality, the argument made is that "outside of the school young people are 'reading' and 'writing' across a new terrain, redefining what literacy might mean"; therefore, schools must meet the demands of students' constant exposure to multiple literacies and redefine the schools' understanding of "what literacy might mean" as well (Jewitt and Kress 2003, 84). Technology in the classroom is not a gimmick, but rather a form of literacy that we have a responsibility to teach.

Trying to keep up electronically with our students is certainly a challenge and we thought that integrating digital technology and multimodal texts in our classrooms, beginning with e-daybooks, would be a great place to begin. North Carolina requires all of its teachers to fulfill the technology requirements within the standard curriculum and to prepare students for a technologically advanced world. Daybooks for us were *the* link between meeting state standards and enjoying the ride.

This chapter explores some of the ideas we have come up with to take the daybook digital and meet some of our students' digital literacy needs. We begin with Shana's idea that makes use of simple tools that we all have access to and builds from there. Read it all and then begin to experiment where you feel comfortable.

Shana's Virtual Daybook: The Mindings Collage

Though North Carolina has technology requirements for teachers and children, the state doesn't necessarily provide us with the latest high-tech gadgets and gizmos to help meet those requirements. I discovered, however, that I could make do by using simple computer programs, such as Microsoft Word or Microsoft FrontPage, and by learning a few tricks from webpage design. I still use my paper-and-pen style daybooks in my classroom because there is something important about feeling the forming of words with our hands. But I have also found potential in my virtual daybook, opening new possibilities for learning. My students often can write faster on the computer, they live virtual lives through chat rooms, and they keep up with the latest gossip through instant messaging.

In my second year of graduate school at UNC Charlotte, I had the pleasure of being introduced to Dr. Sam Watson and his Mindings Collage. Sam is the founder of the UNC Charlotte Writing Project and a dear friend of all the authors of this book. I met Sam in a course about teacher research. On one of the first days of class, he presented us with a disk that contained the core of the collage—a *home* page designed with a collection of circles that looks sort of like a thinking map, each circle having a distinct purpose and place for our writing. He wanted us to use the collage in order to help us see how our thoughts webbed, or minded, together. After hearing his explanation of the collage, I sat there with an obvious *huh?* look on my face. It wasn't until I got home, put the disk in my computer, and began playing with the collage that I started to see what Sam was asking us to do and how it would eventually work for me as a student. I found that the notes and coding I would put in my daybook to connect ideas worked equally well with the links and pages that Sam created in the collage. The main difference was that instead of following *turn to page 59* or trying to remember what my *remember this* note meant, I could simply follow the links created within my collage to see how I was thinking that day.

▶ Hyperlinks: Creating the Connection

The Mindings Collage provides students with a place not only to collect all of their thoughts and ideas, like the daybook does, but it also goes one step further by connecting these ideas in a virtual web on the computer using hyperlinks. A hyperlink is a special area, a link in a document that the user activates by clicking the mouse (when on a webpage) or selects by hitting *control* plus clicking the mouse (when using Microsoft Word). I'll describe how to create hyperlinks a little later, but first I want to describe how the Mindings Collage helped me make connections that I had never seen in my writing.

After taking time to explore all the pages on Sam's collage disk and their purposes, I began to write in the collage. I wanted to get some ideas down about a book I was thinking of writing. Based on Sam's descriptions, it made sense for me to start writing entries on the *trails for blazing* page. From the home page, I clicked on the <blaze> link, which opened the *trails for blazing* page. (To add new entries, I'd move the cursor to the next free line on the *trails for blazing* page and date the start of my entry for that day, just as we do in our daybooks.) Sometimes when I was typing, halfway through my "blaze" I might be reminded of something I read recently that related to my book ideas. That's when I would start making hyperlink connections between blaze pages; at the end of my entry or beside a thought that caused me to think of my recent reading, for example, I created a hyperlink titled <midst>. (See Figure 6–1.)

After I created the hyperlink and then clicked on it, the *a reading I'm in the midst of* page opened up; I added the date for this entry here as well, and continued with my thoughts about how my book ideas related to a certain reading. Now what if there were a quote from the reading that I didn't want to lose? I could create a <quotes> link on the *a reading I'm in the midst of* page, and my thoughts and writing would continue on the *my commonplaces* page. And while I was on that page, I suddenly needed to write an introductory paragraph for the book I've been thinking of, so I made an <exploring> link, which took me to the *an alley I'm exploring* page. Just by adding hyperlinks to each page, my thoughts about one subject—the book I was contemplating—were organized and linked among the categories in the Mindings Collage.

Although the collage, with all its hyperlinks, may seem dizzying at first, it has the potential for amazing results. As any teacher knows, it is difficult for students

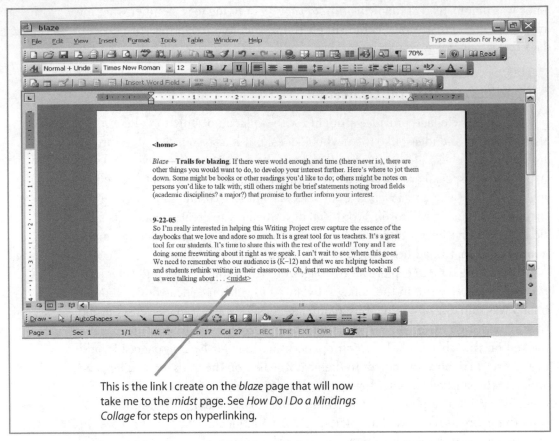

This is the link I create on the *blaze* page that will now take me to the *midst* page. See *How Do I Do a Mindings Collage* for steps on hyperlinking.

Figure 6–1. *Shana's blaze page in her Mindings Collage that sows hyperlinks to other pages.*

to understand how their own minds work, much less to figure out how to capture them in a way that is useful for learning. The Mindings Collage captures our thinking by providing places for all aspects of our thinking. The best part is that students are organizing their ideas and putting them in writing so that ultimately they can examine and learn from seeing how they think. After using the collage as a student, I started to recognize patterns dependent on my purpose for writing that day. If I knew I needed to work on an assignment, then I most likely was always going to toggle between one of the readings pages—<between> or <midst>—and the <exploring> page. However, on a day that I wanted to write with no real agenda in mind, I often drifted between <wind>, <compass>, <myself>, and <what>. To this day I use the collage as an alternative to or change from my daybook. It opens me up to new ways of thinking because I feel free to start writing wherever I want and on whatever I want. Yet, I always wind up focusing on something specific and useful because my ideas have been organized by the collage. The greatest part of all is that I don't feel like *I'm* the one organizing and shaping my thoughts even though I am; it's like some unique relationship is formed between my fingers typing on the keys and the mindings of the collage.

▶ The Home Page

The *home* page of Sam's Mindings Collage works like any homepage on an Internet website except it is a Microsoft Word file. It is the place I start from each time I want to "mind" my thoughts. The page contains twelve various shaped circles and one text box each with a specific title, or hyperlink, which then connects to the page for that title, just like a website. (See Figure 6–2.) The titles and appropriate <links> on the *home* page are *trails for blazing* <blaze>, *readings I'm*

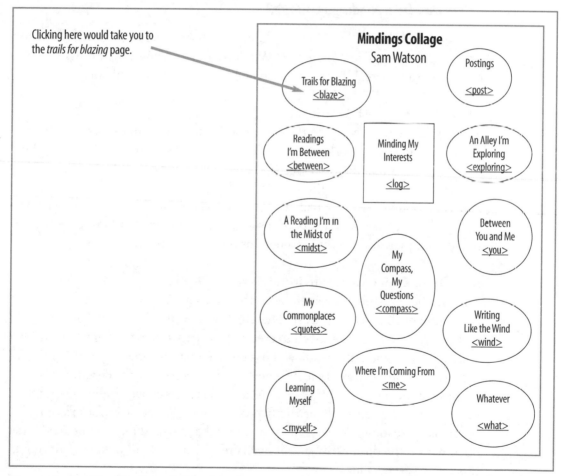

Figure 6–2 *The Mindings Collage home page.*

between <between>, a reading I'm in the midst of <midst>, my commonplaces <quotes>, learning myself <myself>, my compass my questions <compass>, where I'm coming from <me>, whatever <what>, writing like the wind <wind>, between you and me <you>, an alley I'm exploring <exploring>, postings <post>, and minding my interest(s) <log>.

❱ The Mindings Pages

After examining the *home* page, I point and click on each bubble and its link to learn what thoughts that page was created to hold. Although each page has a distinct purpose and description, I found that I could adapt the pages to fit my needs and thoughts as a writer, just like I do in the daybook. (See Figures 6–3a and 6–3b.)

❱ How Do I Do a Mindings Collage?

To create a collage of any sort, I recommend using Microsoft Word, Microsoft FrontPage, or equivalent programs. Whatever program you use, it must have the capability to hyperlink documents, so make sure this is possible before starting.

Step One: Create a Homepage.
The first thing to do is create the homepage from which your students will start each time they go to work and write. In Microsoft Word or FrontPage, create a new document and then decide what pages are needed for the collage. In my classroom, I begin with *reflections on readings*, *reflections on our class*, *connections*, and *golden lines*. I then create the physical links to those pages, or what the students will physically click on in order to get to the page. I have used a combination of pictures, shapes, and text for the links on the homepage.

Step Two: Create the individual pages.
The number one thing to remember is that you can't create a hyperlink to a page or document that does not exist. Therefore, after you decide on what pages will make up your collage, you need to create those pages. Since I begin with having students write about the readings I assign, the first document I create is the *reflections on readings* page. I create a new document, type a brief description of the purpose of the page—in this case, to reflect on their assigned readings—and then save it using the same title as the hyperlink on the homepage (for example, reflections on readings.doc). Again, remember that a hyperlink can't be made to a document if the document has not been created and saved, so make sure you do this before proceeding.

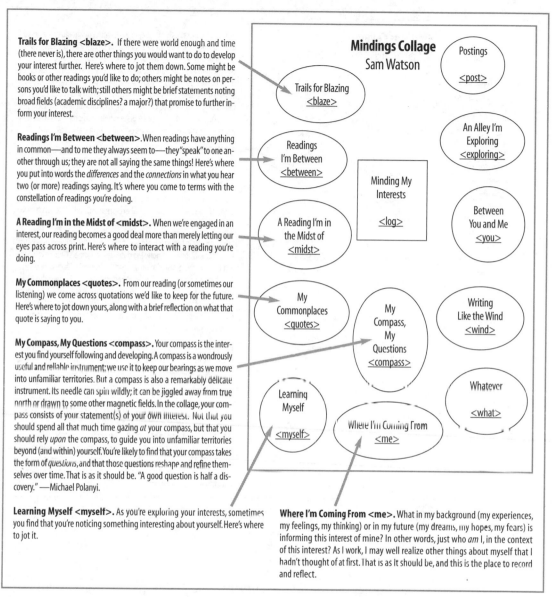

Trails for Blazing <blaze>. If there were world enough and time (there never is), there are other things you would want to do to develop your interest further. Here's where to jot them down. Some might be books or other readings you'd like to do; others might be notes on persons you'd like to talk with; still others might be brief statements noting broad fields (academic disciplines? a major?) that promise to further inform your interest.

Readings I'm Between <between>. When readings have anything in common—and to me they always seem to—they "speak" to one another through us; they are not all saying the same things! Here's where you put into words the *differences* and the *connections* in what you hear two (or more) readings saying. It's where you come to terms with the constellation of readings you're doing.

A Reading I'm in the Midst of <midst>. When we're engaged in an interest, our reading becomes a good deal more than merely letting our eyes pass across print. Here's where to interact with a reading you're doing.

My Commonplaces <quotes>. From our reading (or sometimes our listening) we come across quotations we'd like to keep for the future. Here's where to jot down yours, along with a brief reflection on what that quote is saying to you.

My Compass, My Questions <compass>. Your compass is the interest you find yourself following and developing. A compass is a wondrously useful and reliable instrument; we use it to keep our bearings as we move into unfamiliar territories. But a compass is also a remarkably delicate instrument. Its needle can spin wildly; it can be jiggled away from true north or drawn to some other magnetic fields. In the collage, your compass consists of your statement(s) of your own interest. Not that you should spend all that much time gazing *at* your compass, but that you should rely *upon* the compass, to guide you into unfamiliar territories beyond (and within) yourself. You're likely to find that your compass takes the form of *questions*, and that those questions reshape and refine themselves over time. That is as it should be. "A good question is half a discovery." —Michael Polanyi.

Learning Myself <myself>. As you're exploring your interests, sometimes you find that you're noticing something interesting about yourself. Here's where to jot it.

Where I'm Coming From <me>. What in my background (my experiences, my feelings, my thinking) or in my future (my dreams, my hopes, my fears) is informing this interest of mine? In other words, just who *am* I, in the context of this interest? As I work, I may well realize other things about myself that I hadn't thought of at first. That is as it should be, and this is the place to record and reflect.

Figure 6–3a *The Mindings Collage home page with Sam Watson's descriptions for each Mindings page.*

Step Three: Create the hyperlinks.

After you have created and saved all the pages for the collage, all you have to do is create the hyperlinks to those pages from the homepage. There are several ways to perform the hyperlink function, so use whichever works best.

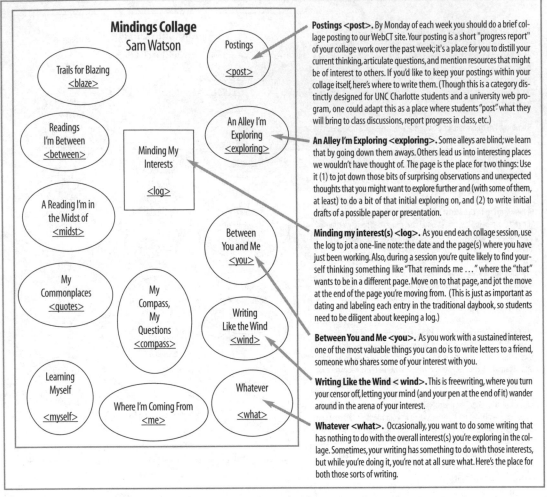

Mindings Collage
Sam Watson

Trails for Blazing <blaze>

Readings I'm Between <between>

Minding My Interests <log>

A Reading I'm in the Midst of <midst>

My Commonplaces <quotes>

My Compass, My Questions <compass>

Learning Myself <myself>

Where I'm Coming From <me>

Postings <post>

An Alley I'm Exploring <exploring>

Between You and Me <you>

Writing Like the Wind <wind>

Whatever <what>

Postings <post>. By Monday of each week you should do a brief collage posting to our WebCT site. Your posting is a short "progress report" of your collage work over the past week; it's a place for you to distill your current thinking, articulate questions, and mention resources that might be of interest to others. If you'd like to keep your postings within your collage itself, here's where to write them. (Though this is a category distinctly designed for UNC Charlotte students and a university web program, one could adapt this as a place where students "post" what they will bring to class discussions, report progress in class, etc.)

An Alley I'm Exploring <exploring>. Some alleys are blind; we learn that by going down them aways. Others lead us into interesting places we wouldn't have thought of. The page is the place for two things: Use it (1) to jot down those bits of surprising observations and unexpected thoughts that you might want to explore further and (with some of them, at least) to do a bit of that initial exploring on, and (2) to write initial drafts of a possible paper or presentation.

Minding my interest(s) <log>. As you end each collage session, use the log to jot a one-line note: the date and the page(s) where you have just been working. Also, during a session you're quite likely to find yourself thinking something like "That reminds me ..." where the "that" wants to be in a different page. Move on to that page, and jot the move at the end of the page you're moving from. (This is just as important as dating and labeling each entry in the traditional daybook, so students need to be diligent about keeping a log.)

Between You and Me <you>. As you work with a sustained interest, one of the most valuable things you can do is to write letters to a friend, someone who shares some of your interest with you.

Writing Like the Wind < wind>. This is freewriting, where you turn your censor off, letting your mind (and your pen at the end of it) wander around in the arena of your interest.

Whatever <what>. Occasionally, you want to do some writing that has nothing to do with the overall interest(s) you're exploring in the collage. Sometimes, your writing has something to do with those interests, but while you're doing it, you're not at all sure what. Here's the place for both those sorts of writing.

Figure 6–3b   *The Mindings Collage home page with Sam Watson's descriptions for each Mindings page.*

Option 1

1. On your homepage, move the cursor to the text or picture for the link.
2. Go to *Insert* in the main menu, click on *Hyperlink*, click on or type in name of document to be hyperlinked, and click *OK*.

Option 2

1. On your homepage, move the cursor to the text or picture for the link.
2. Click on the *Hyperlink* shortcut on the toolbar (it's a picture of the world with a chain link), click on or type in name of document to be hyperlinked, and click *OK*.

Option 3

1. On your homepage, move the cursor to the text or picture for the link.
2. Right-click the mouse, click on *Hyperlink*, click on or type in name of document to be hyperlinked, and click *OK*.

▶ *E-Daybooks Across the Curriculum*

Minding Collages can morph into e-daybooks across the curriculum, including Math Mindings Collages, Social Studies Mindings Collages, and Elementary Mindings Collages. (See Figures 6–4, 6–5, and 6–6.)

Math Mindings Collage: New Concepts and Theories

Each week you are introduced to new math concepts that build off the previous week's work. This page is where to keep definitions, examples, questions, and so on that arise as we develop our understanding of these concepts.

Math Mindings Collage: Chart and Graph Work

Your work in this class often takes a visual form—charts, graphs, diagrams, and so on. *Chart and Graph Work* is where you can work and play with making these

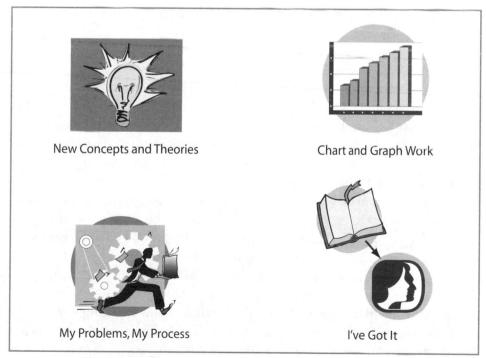

New Concepts and Theories

Chart and Graph Work

My Problems, My Process

I've Got It

Figure 6–4 *A math Mindings Collage.*

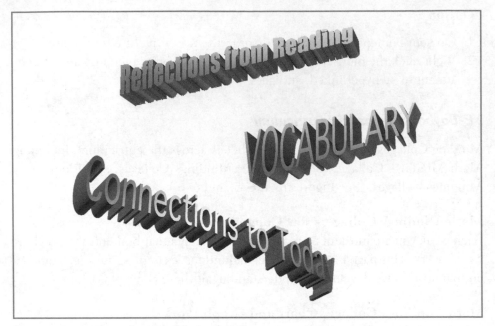

Figure 6–5 *A social studies Mindings Collage.*

visuals using the computer. Be sure to include your process and the steps you took to create each visual.

Math Mindings Collage: My Problems, My Process

As we work through new concepts, new math problems, and new formulas, we will experience our processes and problems differently. This page is the place to write through as well as work through your process work. Additionally, questions or things that are still unclear to you should be noted and used in class discussions.

Math Mindings Collage: I've Got it

Just as it is important for us to note the problems and concepts we have questions about, it is also just as important and helpful to make note of when we finally get it. *I've Got It* is a place to share your triumphs and reflect on how you got there. What steps in your process seemed to work for you and which ones didn't? How will you apply this the next time you struggle or get stuck with a problem?

Social Studies Mindings Collage: Reflections from Reading

You are responsible for all the assigned reading, and it is important for you to actively participate in your reading. *Reflections from Reading* is a place to keep notes,

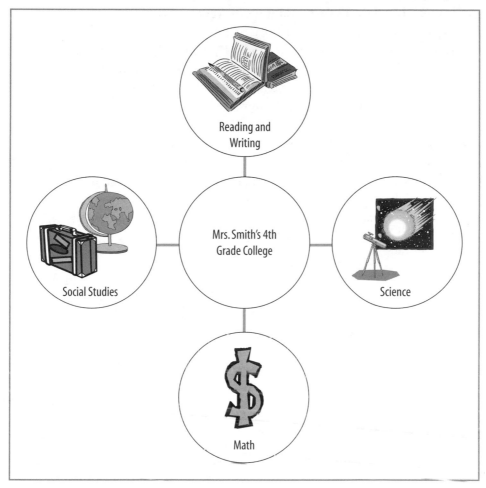

Figure 6–6 *An elementary Mindings Collage.*

reflections, and comments on your reading. You may create double-entry journals using the *column* feature in Word, record and respond to important passages, or whatever illustrates that you are participating with the text.

Social Studies Mindings Collage: Vocabulary
In this class we will encounter many new words and events, so this page is the place to keep up with your expanding vocabulary. Record words, events, dates (assigned as well those you discover on your own), and their corresponding definitions and important details. Additionally, you should look for connections among your reading, new words, and what they mean to you and your understanding of both.

Social Studies Mindings Collage: Connections to Today

History tells us a great deal about where we come from, but it also has direct connections and effects on our lives today. As you find current events, *Connections to Today* is the place to record those events, respond to them, and make connections between the past and the present. Do you see events repeating themselves? How can we learn from our past?

Elementary Mindings Collage

An elementary classroom is a great place for a collage to flourish. Because of all the subject areas covered in an elementary class, the collage could include a hyperlink to each subject on the homepage. The link then leads to another homepage for each subject, and subsequent links branch off from there. In other words, there could be several minicollages within the main collage.

Ultimately, a collage is only useful if the teacher has asked, "What do I want my students to learn?" The page hyperlinks signal what the teacher values and what she wants her students to "mind." For Mindings Collages to function as e-daybooks, students need consistent access to computers either within the classroom or in a computer lab, and the teacher must make time available for students to think and learn in this way. One thing is for certain: It meets the "cool" standard.

connection Grades 4–12

We recognize that Sam Watson created the Mindings Collage for his college students. However, the key ideas behind the collage—*providing students with a way to map and make connections with their thinking*—are applicable across grade levels and subject areas. Shana's visuals of and descriptions for sample collages for a high school math class, a middle school social studies class, and an elementary class illustrate the adaptability of this tool.

The best place to start is to create a collage of your own that works for you personally as a writer.

Tony uses an almost exact replica of Sam's collage with his fourth graders. The only real difference is that Shana, as a graduate student, was able to jump in and begin making sense of each page, while Tony spends a week explaining and discussing with his students what might go on the *trails for blazing* page. He asks his students to "play around with that page" and produce writing for that page only. Then the next week he introduces another page, and students begin exploring, writing, and linking to the new page.

Collages can be as simple or as complicated as you want. The point is that it makes sense for your classroom and your students.

Tony's Community Daybook: The Class Blog

I still use my composition book daybook for most of my class day, but I've added a way of making some of the thinking and reflecting that happens within the daybook public. I created a class blog called Go Furthur where my students can stretch out our discussion and continue our daybook work. I've explained to my students that it's spelled *furthur* rather than further in honor of the 1960s bus that Ken Kesey and his merry band of Pranksters used because I want my students, like the band, to move to the next level in their thinking, to connect with each other and to see that their thoughts are important and can make a difference. The beauty of the blog is that all of these wonderful thoughts are not only available for each of the students in my class to see and respond to each day, but are also archived automatically so that we can keep a history. We can return to any entry at any time to track our thinking and learning.

The first priority for setting up a classroom blog is safety. You must find a safe blog space and get approval from school administrators to activate the blog. To view possible blog sites, use a search engine, such as Google, type in *blogs* and see what comes up. Some that I've used are Blogger (www.blogger.com) and Edu Blog (http//uniblogs.org), but there are many, many more on the Internet. Look for privacy features that do not allow public access, but rather enable only subscribers (the students) to access the blog. Privacy features ensure that students can safely write and respond to each other with supervision by the teacher.

The next step for our blog was to set up several sections where students could write for and to each other. Currently our sections are *class meeting*, *novel discussion*, and *it's story time*. Like Shana's Mindings Collage pages, these sections help focus students' thinking and writing.

After the setup phase, the blog serves as a community daybook. I give different students access to our community daybook blog at different points each day: during our process writing time, while I'm conducting my readaloud in the afternoon, and at the end of the day while we're all completing our daily reflections prior to dismissal. Students are free to post in any of the sections during their time on the blog. At the end of the day, I quickly read through all the posts for that day. I also use this time to post comments and questions to individuals as well as the class in general to keep the discussion flowing. Students look forward to getting back onto the blog to see what I wrote in response to their thoughts, but the thing they look forward to the most is the chance to read each other's ideas.

When I started the project I was concerned about how tuned in to each other's thoughts the students would be when they got their chance to blog. Would they really listen to each other or would they just see the time as an opportunity to hear themselves talk? Like most new things I try in the classroom, I had to learn to relax and trust my students' abilities to display their thinking electronically. After the first day of blogging their responses to a novel we were reading in class, depending on the section of the novel the students chose to read and respond to, their posts ranged from probing questions to revealing emotional responses. However, I continually bring up blog discussions in class in order to highlight powerful conversations, coach students in ways to create more effective postings, and address any general issues that may arise. Below are a few excerpts from our class blog; the first is an exchange between two students from the *novel discussion* section, a section set up for students to continue discussions about the novels they are reading.

> *Al Capone is a very interesting and I love ALL of the people in the story.*
> *But Piper (from my piont of vew) is rather rood and mean and I assume*
> *that she does nothing her daddy (the wardent) tell's her to.*
> *Moose seems like he follows the RULES but Piper always messes*
> *him up. I think Moose is a nice person but if someone messes*
> *with his temper he go's OFF.*
> —HOPE

The next example is from the *it's story time* section. This section is set up for students to stretch out the discussions we have about a novel I'm reading aloud to them.

> *I am looking forward to you finishing this book is funny, bragful, and smart.*
> *I wonder what the end is going to be like?! Will KATE GET AWAY FROM*
> *THIS PRISON OF SMARTNESS!!!!!!!. I like when you make voices for*
> *each person!!!!!! I don't have any connections with this story. Will Kate pull*
> *her grades up. WILL GORIGIE EVER GROW!!!!!!!!!! In this story the boy*
> *said his mother was attacked by the can man but she attacked the can man.*
> *What do you think the author was thinking when he wrote this book??!!*
> *SEE YOU MONDAY!!!!*
> *P.S that book is long you may not finish it to the end of the year!!!!!!!*
> *You are the best teacher ever!!!!!!!1*
> —AMBER

> *If I were dealing with a lady like Cornellia I would just act like the real me.*
> *I am sorry but I have to let out all of my feelings about some people in Story*
> *Time. WARNING! Some of these feelings might be too powerful for*
> *children ages 6 and under so if a kid 6 or under wants to read this please*
> *have some parental guidance. I am just playing!!! But I am not playing*
> *when I say prepare yourself!! I would . . . kick Cornellia in the knee, push*

all of the teachers, and make them fall, and punch George in the face for putting me into this whole stinkin' mess in the first place. No offence George, but still I would of done it. And I feel sorry for Ma, Pa, and June. Well, it's not my problem I don't go to a school with mushroom kids and my teachers are not trying to rule the minds of kids. Or are they? Dum dum duuum! Got to go. I hope you enjoyed my comments. Peace!!!!
—KAYLAH

Wow . . . powerful thoughts about the novel from Kaylah . . . I'm so impressed that you feel comfortable enough to express them!
—MR. EYE

As you can see, the spelling and grammar are not perfect, just like in a paper daybook. Yet, if we read these posts carefully, we can see and feel passion for what is being discussed. We can see the students' voices coming alive on the page. We see students realizing connections, using humor and wit, stating opinions, asking questions. It's a teacher's dream! The blog has provided my students with the opportunity to become better readers and writers by creating

connection Grades 6–12

In many ways Tony's blog is like one dialectical journal that the whole class has a chance to participate in—including Tony! The blog is a great way to get students talking about their reading while the teacher is able to observe, comment on, and contribute to it. The blog is a valuable tool for making public within the school community some of the very best thinking and learning from the daybook. Through blogs, we envision a free-flowing conversation between the blog and the daybook. Since students need to post only once a day, having just a few computers for them to access will work.

Because of the potential for higher-level thinking, blogs are a powerful possibility for older students as well. Since the inception of instant messaging and MySpace, older students typically are using such technologies to communicate with each other. Therefore, they could also blog independently from home or the school library. While this may allow teachers to tap into literacy skills their middle and high school students are already exercising, it is even more important to maintain a private and well-monitored blog. Like Tony and Shana urge, teachers of older students must ensure that they have a clear purpose and intent for taking their daybooks digital. It is well worth it to do thorough research on class blog sites, understand the dynamics of the students, and use the blog responsibly. When all of that is done, not only are we engaging students by working with literacy skills they are already interested in, but we are educating them about how to use them safely and appropriately.

an electronic community daybook as a place where they can meet and have fun sharing their ideas with each other.

Sally's Tech-Savvy Classroom: Daybooks Meet the Digital Age

I'm always having to wrestle down the coach to get the projector to show PowerPoint slides or help a student with algebra so that she, in turn, will show me how she edits digital movies, but it's worth it to see how my students' writing comes alive when daybooks meet the digital age.

The students at my high school are tech-savvy—more tech-savvy than most of their teachers and parents. For projects, they ask over and over if they can make a movie or a slide show and they come to near rebellion if all the project options are "boring paper things." Several years ago I realized that in the technology area I needed either to lead or get out of the way. I decided not to get out of the way. To keep up with my students, I subscribed to a couple of technology publications, became a part of the technology leaders' group in the school system, and embarked on a whole new technological life for me and for daybooks in my classes.

▶ *Getting Students Ready To Go Digital*

Along with pencils, pens, and a daybook, all of my students are required to have a floppy disk or a flash drive. I don't like CD-Rs and CD-RWs because I have found them to be unstable and to go blank or lose all the information, which often is not backed up and is a great loss to the writer. It is little consolation that the manufacturer will replace the faulty CD with a shiny new one. We then create and maintain e-daybooks as multimedia or multimodal means of capturing our thinking and writing. E-daybooks allow students to use their actual voices, photographs from home, and pictures that they draw, all those things that make writing less threatening and more natural. In their e-daybooks, students can digitally record themselves talking about their lives by using digital movie cameras. Students can record their conversation with a friend about something that really matters to them, for example. Digital voice and movie clips can combine into digital stories. Once students see the potential of making an e-daybook, the possibilities are never ending.

▶ *How to Make E-Daybooks*

Student begin by freewriting in any word processing program (I use Microsoft Word because of its versatility and because it's available at my school). As students' stories start emerging, I ask them to take photographs that could serve as illustrations. For the many students without digital cameras or cellphone cameras, I purchase disposable cameras, one for every two students, and allot each student half the exposures on the camera. I take the cameras to the local store and save the photographs onto a CD. We then upload the photographs to the class computer and insert them into their Word documents using the software's *insert* function. When new pictures aren't enough, students bring in old family photographs or drawings they have made that we scan into the computer and insert into the document in the same way as new photos. Some students surf the Internet to find clipart or pictures, always giving credit to sources as real researchers do. The pictures give students motive to revise their writing, to think more deeply about their lives, and to explore memories that, before the pictures, were forgotten.

Instead of using Word, sometimes my students compose their e-daybooks in PowerPoint. They like PowerPoint because it allows the students to easily bring in their own digital material. They import their material into PowerPoint, then sit in front of the computer with a cheap microphone I purchased at the local electronic warehouse and speak into a program I downloaded free from the internet. (One such freeware package is Audacity [http://audacity.sourceforge.net/].) Students can import their voices as sound to accompany their pictures in PowerPoint.

We also use MovieMaker, which makes it possible for us to move photographs and clipart easily from PowerPoint files into a movie. Students bring pictures and documents from home, scan them, and create single pictures or frames of the movie. In other words, the movie is like a slide show, showing one picture at a time. We plug microphones into the computers, and students read their stories while looking at the pictures. MovieMaker makes this process easy. While PowerPoint does accept voiceovers, I prefer movie software because of the versatility of the medium as we move from e-daybooks to the finished product. Movie software (including MovieMaker or Pinnacle for PCs and iMovie for Macs) allow movie clips of students talking about their writing, makes drafts of their stories possible to save, and simplifies importing pictures and art with their voice files. Pinnacle has two audio tracks so that background music can be added to various parts, should the student desire it.

▶ Making E-Daybooks Their Own

Students like to decorate the covers of their conventional daybooks and on the inside paste in photos, ticket stubs, drawings, magazine clippings, and other treasures. The digital daybook allows the same option. They can create an introductory page that is a replica of the cover of their conventional daybook or design a totally digital "cover." Students also like to scan in or photograph pages from their conventional daybooks and add them to the electronic daybook. They are easily retrieved electronically on PowerPoint slides or added to a movie version. At any time they can add or reduce the number of slides in a particular e-daybook section, print out pieces for their conventional daybooks, or move slides from one presentation to another. The only major difference in the two daybooks at this point is that one requires a computer to view it and the other does not.

⟩ Why E-Books Matter

The electronic daybook offers students a way to communicate in more than one dimension. The student who says, "I can see it, but I can't say it," has an option of *seeing it* through pictures and *saying it* by adding story with help from his writing group and his own insights as he views and reviews the images. The student who composes better facing a blank screen than a blank sheet of paper is no longer at a disadvantage. She simply sits at the computer, writes, saves, and prints. The student who needs to talk the story over can use a digital recorder to tell the story, transcribe it, or leave it in voice form and add art to illustrate it. They can write in Word or use other software such as Inspiration, which offers graphic organizer capabilities for students who want to picture and link their thinking, similar to Shana's description of the Mindings Collage. These can be captured as pictures and inserted into the movie or PowerPoint slide show.

⟩ Student Reflections in the E-Daybook: On Trying to Write Like Emily Dickinson

One student in my creative writing class wanted to explore her own poetry by looking carefully at the work of Emily Dickinson, one her favorite poets. She combined various sections from her paper daybook with a PowerPoint presentation to document her growth as a writer. (See Figure 6–7.)

Concluding Thoughts

As with our paper-and-pen daybooks, bringing digital options for writing into our classrooms is another way to meet all learning styles and all types of writers. As Sally has pointed out, technology is a very real part of our students' lives and we either can choose to use it or ignore it, but it will not go away. If we model all other forms of writing for our students, why not model tech-savvy writing? It's not

Exploring Dickinson...

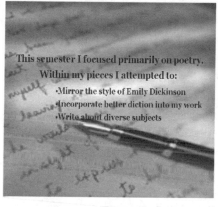

My growth as a writer: Fall 2005

This semester I focused primarily on poetry. Within my pieces I attempted to:

- Mirror the style of Emily Dickinson
- Incorporate better diction into my work
- Write about diverse subjects

I've learned a lot since I started writing poetry. Here's an example of a piece I wrote while a sophomore in Creative Writing I:

THE LIFEBOAT

Love is a lifeboat,
Languidly floundering upon the sea.
Waves crash about my head,
And threaten to prevail.
Thrashing through the icy murk,
I take hold of its side.
Hands reach down and pull me,
Into its serene interior.
My fear is gone with the wind and waves,
I sink into its gentle embrace,
And know the worst is over.

Has obvious problems with rhythm
Shows little organization
Anyone can slap words on a page that sound nice together...
I wanted to write poetry with a definite form
So I turned to the work of Emily Dickinson

My first attempt at writing like Dickinson took pages and pages of editing before it sounded right...

Creeping Mortality

A sickness dwells within my bones
It seems that none can see
I daily hear its morbid tones –
Creeping Mortality

A weakness seems to rule my flesh
Pernicious darkness there
Pervading with a cruel finesse
And leaving blank Despair

The more I read her work, the more I discovered patterns in her writing.
She used inverted word order.
She wrote in iambic meter,
usually with lines of six and eight syllables.
She capitalized common nouns she thought important
(e.g. Love, Death, Adversity, etc.)
She often used dashes to isolate important words or phrases.

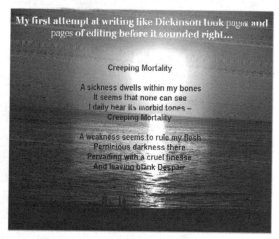

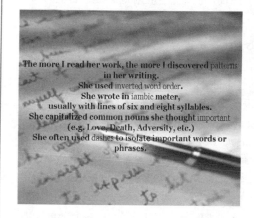

Figure 6–7 *One student's PowerPoint e-daybook about Emily Dickinson.*

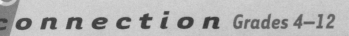

connection Grades 4–12

Concerns or Learning Opportunities?

One of the fears of electronic writing and storage of that writing has been the potential for loss of multiple drafts. The drafts of famous writers—lines scratched through, words edited in or out—that have been preserved in books are valuable to beginning writers in that they see that even the masters must endure considerable agonizing and revision. Our students are required to *save as* draft one, draft two, draft three, and so on, preserving each draft as a separate file. These drafts give students the opportunity to look back at their work and reflect on how they are changing as writers. They also have access to versions of a piece that they can cut and paste into new documents. Students enjoy this ease of movement, and often say that they *hate* copiously retyping or copying an entire section from a paper daybook.

However, the blessing of ease with which students can cut and paste their own writing from one document to another comes with the curse of plagiarizing from the Internet. Plagiarism from the web and the possibility of attack by a cyberpredator always loom as possibilities, but teachers' and students' careful awareness of the threats can minimize them. Since it is easy for anyone to cut and paste material from the web and import it into their own document, it is our responsibility to remind students about voice—their own and that of other, sometimes more articulate authors. Some schools have implemented detective software, such as http://turnitin.com (http://turnitin.com) to ferret out the stolen words. I have found that with high school students and a familiarity with their writing, I know when the voice changes. Simple quote marks around a suspected phrase in the Google box will bring up the original piece. We do have to remind students of the importance of their own words and of documenting sources that they use in service of their own ideas. Researchers of today have the resources of the Internet at their disposal, so our students need to understand how to evaluate those resources and think critically about what they are saying.

In addition to issues of academic integrity, the issues of predators must be addressed when discussing technology. Most schools have filters that make accessing potentially vulgar or problematic sites more difficult. Nonetheless, teachers need to talk to students about the problems of conversing with strangers, especially electronically. Teachers need to warn students to never give out their names or addresses and never give a stranger access to personal pages just because the person "sounds nice" or "seems like a normal kid." These warnings can be transferred to their out-of-school online daybooks as well. Most of our writing students have their own pages on sites such as My Space and Zenga. Over and over we caution students about putting up pictures of themselves, addresses, and telephone numbers. The same rules go for their work in our class on their e-daybooks. Again, we are trying to create critical consumers of all media. We see these potentially problematic issues as yet another opportunity to increase our students' literacy and prepare them for the world outside of our classroom.

a gimmick that will fade as soon as our students get used to the flashing lights and cool equipment. Digital literacy is a very real part of the world our students live in. We have an obligation to show them how to navigate what's available and use it toward their own thinking and learning.

What to Remember About E-Daybooks

Whether or not you are someone who must feel the pen moving across the page in order to write or who feels deprived having to write without a computer, the E-daybook will probably become part of your writing life. We hope you will venture in, using your students as helpful guides.

- Teachers work in e-daybooks too, and model, model, model.

- E-daybooks can make our teaching lives simpler and more complex.

- Students can often help us figure out how to make e-daybooks work in our classrooms.

- E-daybooks can make images and texts speak to one another.

- E-daybooks make critical thinking easier and harder.

- E-daybooks can make thinking public and therefore a part of the community.

- Take the time to properly plan for technology instruction and prepare students as well.

- We don't all have to become Sally in one day. Pick one e-book option and begin there. See where it takes you.

7

Assessing Daybooks
Valuing Process over Product

Self assessment is universal truth.

—Sun Tzu

I
n our classes, where students range from unwilling to get a wrong answer at the risk of affecting a perfect GPA to unwilling to try because over the years the answer has *always* been wrong, what makes the daybook work as a tool for thinking is the fact that it is a safe haven for students to freely explore thoughts without being judged by the literary or academic genius of the teacher. Because we value individual thinking in our students, the daybook contributes to a large percentage of our students' grades. Over the years, we've looked at random pages, counted entries, or required and checked for writing each night. These meth-

The Daybook: Documenting and Enhancing Learning

Peter Johnston's *Knowing Literacy: Constructive Literacy Assessment* (1997) provides the theoretical rationale for our views of assessment. Johnston argues that assessment is human, social, and always interpretative. Students and teachers are coinvestigators of literacy and students need to learn how to assess their own learning and think constructively and critically about it. He reminds us that assessment comes from the Latin word "assidere, meaning to sit alongside" (2). If as teachers we can sit alongside our students, we can show them what they are doing well and help them take control of their own learning. The assessments we describe in this chapter attempt to help students understand what is being valued by the teacher and that they can share in this process of valuing. Peter Elbow (1996) argues that we need always to minimize the untrustworthiness of quantitative writing assessment. He says, "we [as teachers] can assess better…so we must do it less…less will be better" (120). Our practices are based on constructivist views of language and learning, which holds that teachers and students construct knowledge together and that learning takes place through interactions and dialogue. Documenting this kind of learning is what we are doing in this chapter. Assessment should enhance learning, helping students and teachers in the ongoing process of learning together.

ods, however, just were not satisfying. Counting pages or checking for writing made us feel as though what the students were saying did not matter. Assessment was more like surveillance rather than purposeful or meaningful dialogue with our students. Over time each of us has found that the way to value what we do with daybooks is to give the students ownership over the assessment of this important work through reflection.

Karen's Assessment: Creating Reflective Students Bit by Bit

A key component to daybooks is self-assessment. By having their thinking in one central place, students can refer back to their ideas throughout the year. Writers look back over the pages and see progress. Therefore, while I do a variety of spot checking to see what my students are thinking, I don't grade daybooks any longer in the traditional sense. Through various means, I ask my students to reflect on what is happening in their daybooks and document what they see. Students build this reflectiveness over time through daily, weekly, and quarterly assessments. These assessments become as important for growth as the work itself.

▶ Quick Assessment

To keep track of my students' thinking and learning, as I walk around the class-room I informally assess my students all the time. I use the following strategies to keep the task simple:

- I ask students to point me to specific pages to read.

- I ask students to leave their daybooks on their desks open to a specific page.

- I ask students to bring their daybooks to conference and share specific pages with me.

I always look for evidence of student thinking, and I do this by asking students to explain what they're learning. When students engage with me in meaningful conversations about what they are writing or reading, I am satisfied that their daybooks are working and I don't feel the need to give a point value to every page.

▶ Daily Reflection: Exit Sheets

Daily reflections are my method for students to make meaning of the day's events by looking back over the thinking they have done in their daybooks. To accomplish this, I ask them to complete an exit sheet before they leave class each day. When we first begin using exit sheets, students often write the daily agenda off the board, thinking that they are supposed to tell me what we did that day. I have to model for them that I'm not asking for the agenda but that I want them to think about their reactions to activities and what they are taking away from the day. On the exit sheets, I ask students to respond to two statements: *I learned* and *I wonder*. My goal is twofold: I have a quick check on what the students learned and I can figure out if any students need extra assistance in understanding new concepts.

▶ Weekly Reflection

Weekly reflections take twenty to thirty minutes and typically build on students' writing and thinking in their daybooks. Weekly reflections consist of questions that invite students to reflect on themselves as writers or readers and to look analytically at their work in their daybooks. Even if the questions appear difficult, I ease any confusion by discussing what each question means and modeling how to answer. I usually make the reflection a Friday activity.

Throughout the year, I use a variety of reflective questions, depending on what we're studying:

- What prewriting strategies do you use? Why? Tell me how they work for you.

- How did you decide on your topic?

- What are the characteristics of good writing? Is your writing good writing? Why or why not? Use examples from your daybook to illustrate your point.

- Pick out two things you really improved on in your daybook. Sticky-note those places and explain the improvement.

- Are you keeping a topic page? Is it helpful to you? Why or why not?

- How do you determine what needs to be revised? Illustrate using examples from your daybook.

- Are you good at revision? Why or why not? Illustrate with examples from your daybook.

- What revision strategies do you use? Give examples and explanations of how you use them by pointing to examples in your daybook.

- How do you think your daybook would be the same or different from a more experienced writer or a less experienced writer?

- How do you know when your writing is ready to leave your daybook?

- What is your plan for proofreading? Is your plan for proofreading working? Explain. Point to improvements in your paper as evidence that your plan is working.

▶ Quarterly Reflection

Once each quarter I ask students to look back on all the thinking they have recorded in their daybooks. This assessment asks students to look holistically at their work, to look carefully at all the different kinds of writing they have produced, and make a record of their learning. I give each student a handout in order to guide their reflections and ask them to paste it into their daybooks. (See Figure 7–1.)

Reflection gives students control over and responsibility for their writing. It gives them a way of seeing the value of their work and noticing what they are doing and why. It makes them responsible for their growth and learning. Each of

Daybook Reflection

Name _____ Date _____

Look through the writing you did this quarter in your daybook. Answer these two questions:

1. How many days have you written for at least ten minutes on your own? ___

2. Record the number of times you have written a piece that could be classified as:

    ___ autobiography

    ___ biography

    ___ letter

    ___ imaginative narrative

    ___ personal narrative

    ___ fable, folktale, or myth

    ___ play or skit

    ___ research

    ___ contest entry

    ___ personal response to reading

    ___ directions

    ___ character sketch

    ___ setting sketch

    ___ other? Explain _____

Answer these two questions:

1. What did you discover about yourself as a writer?

2. What goals can you set so that you will improve as a writer?

Figure 7–1 *Quarterly Daybook Reflection.*

© 2008 by Lil Brannon et al. from Thinking Out Loud on Paper. *Portsmouth, NH: Heinemann.*

these reflective assessments—the exit sheets, weekly and quarterly reflections—build on each other, giving students practice at looking at their work and a language to speak about what they are doing. Over time, their reflections grow deeper and more meaningful.

Cindy's Daybook Defense: Replacing Tests with Reflective Assessment

The daybook defense has gone a long way to help me bridge the gap between my process- and workshop-based teaching style and assessment. Novel tests and portfolios, along with checking daybooks for numbers of entries or the correctness of a particular entry, seemed to invalidate all I was saying to my students about the importance and value of thinking, risk taking, and finding their own learning style and process.

▶ How the Daybook Defense Came to Be

The disconnect between what I was teaching and the way I was assessing became very clear during the third quarter of the third year I committed to making the daybook the center of our classroom. I was confident that my students understood that I expected them to think carefully and critically about what they were reading and take risks in their writing and thinking. But during a challenging study of *Les Miserables* that, in my mind, should have reinforced the necessity of a safe place to ponder and try out ideas, I collected the students' daybooks and was horrified. Twelve different students from among the three classes had simply copied the summaries and analysis from an online form of a study guide. Ten others had at least used their own words, but also had clearly used a study guide as a reference. My worst nightmare had come true. The daybook had become busywork for these students.

As I pondered what had gone wrong and discussed it with colleagues, the problem became clear: Too many of my students simply were not making a connection between the thinking they were doing in their daybooks and their other assignments. At some point the product certainly had to be assessed, but I didn't want to take the value away from process in order to do that. If I was teaching my students that the process of thinking and authentic original thought was important, I needed to value those things in my assessment.

▶ *What Is a Daybook Defense?*

The daybook defense is a portfolio of sorts in which students defend the idea that they are truly using their daybooks as thinking tools. Students are required to photocopy and highlight evidence of thinking about literature in their daybooks and then reflect in writing about what they are seeing in these artifacts. The letters the students write and the artifacts they collect allow me to meet each student where he or she is and have each one *show* me what they've learned and the progress they have made. It also gives the students practice in writing authentic, well-supported argument.

For me, the daybook defense accomplishes the following goals:

- It makes students accountable for the thinking I require of them in their daybooks.

- It gives students space to access their own thinking, learning, process, and progress.

- It helps students become reflective learners.

- It enables me to access learning, thinking, process, and progress without freezing student voices.

- It enables students to see the information their daybooks hold for extended pieces of writing.

- It helps students work toward building a case and defending it in writing.

The assignment below is an example of a daybook defense my students put together at the beginning of the year. *Color of Water* and *The Great Gatsby* were summer reading assignments made by another teacher. The students were required to keep double-entry journals (see Chapter 5) for *Color of Water* and do color marking for literary patterns, in which they choose three passages, color code the literary elements found there, and then discuss the purpose of those elements, for *The Great Gatsby*. We studied *Cold Sassy Tree* as a class, but students were required to choose a method, or several methods, of writing-to-learn to study the novel, prepare for class discussion, and extend from discussion at the end of each day. At the end of the quarter, students would be choosing their own topics for a literary analysis paper dealing with two or more of these works, so the information in their daybooks would help them form and write about these topics. Daybook defenses also reflect and assess topics and analysis skills that students are working with in the course of a study.

DAYBOOK DEFENSE/PORTFOLIO

Color of Water, The Great Gatsby, and Cold Sassy Tree

Directions: Collect the following in a *paper folder*. The reflective essay must be typed. The remaining pieces of the portfolio may be photocopied from your daybook (what I would do), or typed. *Ripped daybook pages will receive no credit!*

1. Reflective Essay: Explain how the items you have chosen show growth in your ability to think about literature. Collect bits of writing and thinking that may be used for major papers, presentations, and projects in the future. Be sure to discuss your reasons for choosing each item in the portfolio.

2. *Color of Water*: Choose an excerpt from your summer assignment.

3. *The Great Gatsby*: Choose your best example of color marking.

4. *Cold Sassy Tree*: Choose four excerpts from writing-to-learn, one from each reading assignment.

5. Class Writings: Choose four examples of in-class writing.

6. Other: Choose anything else from your daybook that shows your growth as a reader, thinker, and writer.

The next daybook defense assignment is for an International Baccalaureate junior class, and therefore more complex than the previous assignment. It takes place in class because of the workload that students were experiencing in other subjects at that time. As an in-class assessment, it reflects all of the concepts students worked with and explored in an in-depth study of *Like Water for Chocolate*. At the beginning of the study, I told students that they would need to explore the topics evident in the daybook defense assignment. As they read each section of the novel, students recorded their thinking on these topics through writing-to-learn techniques (see Chapter 5) and then tested and honed that thinking through small-group discussion and seminars.

DAYBOOK DEFENSE

Like Water for Chocolate

Answer the following on notebook paper and turn in at the end of the period. Be sure that *all* answers are well thought out, well supported, and organized. This may require some drafting. Remember that I am far more concerned with your thinking processes and your attempts to practice independent literary analysis here than with *perfect* analysis. However, I *do* want to see you supporting all statements and generalizations.

1. You were asked to work with the encryptions in the recipes in this novel. How did you use your daybook *outside* of class to do accomplish this task? Support your statement by detailing your most successful recipe study from the last assigned section of the novel. (Please remember that questioning is a significant strategy as long as the questions show more study than simply "What is the purpose of this recipe?")

2. You were asked to view this novel through the lens of social commentary on the Mexican Revolution. How did you use your daybook *outside* of class to think about this issue? Support your statement by detailing your most successful study on this issue in *one* of the chapters from the last section you were assigned. Remember the importance of questioning.

3. You were asked to consider the elements of magical realism in this novel. How did you use your daybook *outside* of class to think about this issue? What did you decide about the legitimacy of the terms *magical realism* versus *realism* or *fantasy*? Support your statements by detailing your most successful study of the issue in *one* of the chapters in the last section you were assigned.

At the end of the study, students were required to complete a fifteen-minute oral commentary presentation on one of the books we read in the first semester. The daybook defense reminded them once more of the wealth of information they had in their daybooks to help in the creation of that presentation. Note that students are asked to write from the last section of the novel they were assigned; prior sections were discussed in class after the students worked with them and learned what they needed to do to enhance their study. Their study of the last section was not discussed in class, so it is a better reflection of their own thinking and study skills, including the decision to discuss their thoughts with other students outside of class.

When introducing this kind of assessment for the first time, teachers may choose to work with one of these concepts in the study of a novel such as social commentary on the Mexican Revolution or the identity of and legitimacy of the term *magical realism*. That one concept could be broken down into more manageable parts and then built upon. The key is to create a challenging study that stretches students, whatever their abilities, and then create an assessment that rewards that risk taking and stretching rather than searching for a right or regurgitated answer. The daybook defense assessment values the process through which students reach their conclusions over one right answer while making room for individual differences in writing styles and processes.

▶ Challenges

I have been thrilled with the daybook defense's replacement of unit tests and daybook checks as major grades in my classroom. However, there are some challenges to the practice.

First, putting the daybook defense together can seem time-consuming to students. I agree that it is, but it takes no more time than what we would expect students to spend studying for a test. It is more difficult for students to talk themselves out of spending the necessary time when they have something to collect and turn in than it is when the product happens in the classroom. It is also more meaningful than memorizing and regurgitating information. If students are particularly busy, a way to alleviate that issue is to make the daybook defense an in-class assessment as in the second example above.

The second challenge is a trust and control issue for me as a teacher. Because students get to pick their best work, I worry that what I see in the collection is all some of them have done. I have to remind myself that some of them simply don't need to do as much as others to reach our class goals. These students often are quicker and pick things up more naturally. The ones who haven't put in the necessary thought and time into their daybook defenses show it in their lack of understanding and the lack of depth of analysis in their writing. Each student has a different process that works for her or him. Not only do I need to help my students find that process, but I must trust it as well.

Tony's Assessment: The Daybook Defense Goes Elementary and Cross-Curricular

Like Cindy, I struggled to find a way to hold my students accountable for the thinking going on in their daybooks. Before this current school year started, I took a long look at what I was doing when it came to grading my students and I wanted to change it. I wanted my grading to reflect what I value most in the classroom: process, thinking, risk taking, and reflection. I spend a great deal of time explaining these four concepts to my students early in the year. I also provide students with opportunities to experience all four the very first week of school.

As the year progresses, I give my students daybook defense assignments at the end of units, such as in mathematics and when they finish novel studies with classmates (see below). The daybook defense has been the answer to my prayers in terms of how to hold my students accountable for what goes on in their daybooks. I don't grade the actual work in the daybooks, rather I grade their ability to talk about their learning by reflecting on the assignments from their daybook.

NOVEL DAYBOOK DEFENSE

OK, you've just finished reading a great piece of literature and now it's time to show what you've learned from the experience. A daybook defense is a written assignment in which you use the ideas in your daybook to defend what you've learned.

Part 1: Novel Discussions

One of the great things about a novel study is that you get to talk to others about what you're reading. After each discussion, I asked you to reflect on what went on in your daybook. Go back through the reflections you wrote to see what you liked and what you learned. Write me a letter that explains what you liked and what you learned as a result of sitting with your classmates talking about your novel. Make sure that you use specific details from your daybook reflections in your letter to me. When I'm finished reading your letter, I want to know how important the discussions you had were to your understanding and enjoyment of the novel. This part of the daybook defense will be graded on a three-point scale; that means the best score you can get is a *3*.

Part 2

In Part 1 of your daybook defense, you wrote about how talking in your discussion groups helped you learn. In Part 2, you'll look at the products you created (double-entries, bookmarks, body biographies), and you'll write to me about how creating these products helped you. Here's what I need you to do:

1. Look at the two body biographies that you drew in your daybook and the bookmarks that you made.

2. Look over the writing you brought to your literature circle, along with the double-entries in your daybook.

3. Pick items from your daybook and write a letter to me that explains how creating these helped you better understand the novel and the characters in it.

4. Make sure that you use specific details from the two items you choose.

When I'm finished reading your letter, I want to know how creating and using each item helped you while you read the novel. This part of the daybook defense will be graded on a three-point scale, meaning the best you can do is a *3*.

Part 3

In Part 3, you will analyze the sticky-note responses you made while reading your novel. They provide footprints to your thinking if you examine them. Here's what I want you to do:

1. Take the sticky notes out of the novel and place them in your daybook in numerical order based on the pages each note came from.

2. Write me a letter that describes:
   - Which type of response did you make the most? What does this say about you as a reader?
   - Which sticky note got you thinking the most? How did this happen?
   - Which sticky note helped you the most? In what way did it help you?

When I'm finished reading your letter, I want to know how using the sticky notes affected you as a reader. This letter will be graded on a three-point scale; the best you can score is a *3*.

GEOMETRY DAYBOOK DEFENSE

We're at the end of the geometry unit. On one sheet of loose-leaf paper, please write me a letter than explains the following:

■ Describe what it means to translate (slide), rotate (turn), and reflect (flip) a geometric figure. Use the practice sheets we did in class that are pasted in your daybook as the basis for your descriptions.

■ Explain your understanding of how to use coordinate points on a grid. Use the practice sheets we used in class as the basis of your explanation.

■ Identify *intersecting*, *parallel*, and *perpendicular lines*, *line segments*, and their *midpoints*. Use the class math sheets in your daybook to identify each.

Your daybook defense will be graded based on how well you describe, explain, and identify the information above based on the International Baccalaureate rubric for thinking and writing we've used all year.

c o n n e c t i o n Grades 4–12

Though Cindy and Tony work with very different grade levels of students, their goals for assessment are the same. Both teachers strive to make their students aware of their own thinking and the process by which they do it. Both teachers want to keep their students in touch with the wonderful things that are happening in their daybooks as they think and learn, and both teachers strive to value all of those things in their assessment of the students and their daybooks. The key is finding the appropriate way to help students in any given classroom access the thinking in their daybooks, see the value of that thinking, and articulate that value.

Lil's Challenge to the Daybook Defense

While I have always asked students to copy out certain pieces from their daybook and reflect on their thinking and learning just as Cindy, Karen, and Tony do, I am reluctant to call this activity a *daybook defense*. For some reason, it makes me think of military imagery, as if we are asking students to defend their work against the onslaught of a bad grade. Instead, I call my daybook assessments *a time for reflection*, and I ask my students to give me examples of their best thinking. For instance, I might ask them to reflect on some of the following:

- A piece of writing done in class that was particularly important to you. Explain your selection.

- A piece that will show me who you are as a learner. Explain.

- A piece that will show me who you are as a collaborator. Explain.

- A piece that demonstrates who you are as an analytic thinker. Explain.

- An instance that shows you as a risk-taker. Explain.

The possibilities are endless and typically follow the contours of our class discussion and class activities. Once I get these reflections, I use a rubric to guide my assessment. (See Figure 7–2.) I use the sections of the rubric that are blank to record my thinking and respond specifically to the students and their work.

Shana builds on Cindy's and Tony's version of the daybook defense, combined with Lil's time for reflection daybook assessment, and creates an elaborate portfolio assessment that asks students to recognize the important process components they get from their daybooks.

Shana's Use of the Portfolio to Make the Daybook the Center of Final Course Assessment

When I first asked my students to capture all their thinking and writing in daybooks, their concerns for their grades became an even bigger issue because they did not see the purpose of the daybooks in the long run. Portfolios became my answer to that problem, and they have helped me shift the focus and culture of my classroom away from grades or products and toward something more—the process and development of writers.

	Awesome!	Fine Work—What I Expected	OK, but…	Is this your daybook?
Evidence of Responses to Readings				
Involvement with Class Activities				
Growth as a Thinker				
Honest Attempt to Keep Daybook				

Figure 7–2 *Lil's rubric for daybook assessment.*

My first attempt at integrating the portfolio into the entire class assessment was a major flop, but I had good intentions. I wanted my students to literally *see* all the work they had created in one semester, in an effort to get them to appreciate all the process work I had required of them in their daybooks and how that developed and influenced their prewriting, drafts, final pieces, and reflections. The problem was that I did not design the entire course around the daybook, but rather I made the culminating portfolio simply a binder with all their "stuff" in it. I did have them write a final reflection, and in it I wanted them to examine all their work from their daybook and writing assignments. I wanted them to respond in some prolific way that would help me know how all of the papers and daybook work they had collected in the binder fit together and taught them something. But I did nothing that would help them understand those connections during the semester because I hadn't designed the daybook writing and writing assignments to really connect with each other. So what I wound up with was about eighty massive three-ring binders with a few dividers in each and some haphazard and ill-constructed reflections in which my students tried their best to make sense out of what lay before them. Essentially, I wound up with no productive way to read them because I had not given my students or myself any real direction or purpose for assessing the daybook via a portfolio.

▶ Presenting the Portfolio

It wasn't until I took the UNC Charlotte Writing Project Summer Invitational and completed my *own* portfolio, reflecting on my daybook work, that I finally figured out how to make it effective in my classroom. Just as the facilitators did with us during the Writing Project, from the first day of class I make the purpose clear to my students: *Everything* you do in this class is important and crucial to your development as a writer and thinker, and the portfolio is going to be evidence of that.

For my classes, I use portfolios not only to assess the daybook but also to assess all their process work for writing assignments, polished and final writing assignments, and reflections throughout the class. One section of the portfolio in particular captures the students' daybook work: *Folder 1: Daybook Entries and In-Class Writing*. My class syllabus provides a general overview of what my students are responsible for in their portfolio. Based on the syllabus, the students realize from the beginning of the year that their daybooks are important and vital to their development as writers and will be a significant part of their final portfolio. Here is the description of the daybook portion of the portfolio:

Folder 1: *Daybook Entries and In-Class Writing*

Throughout the semester, you are expected to write weekly notes/meditations/letters/thought pieces in response to your readings, writings, and to the class. You will maintain a daybook in order to write your thoughts and understanding of the contents of this course on a weekly basis. I expect you to read, write, observe, participate, respond, think, and feel. Above all, I expect you to share with the class whatever insights and/or problems this class provokes in you. The daybook will help you fulfill this expectation and show evidence of your journey this semester. You will need your daybook in class every day.

▶ Grading the Portfolio

As for the actual grading, I do assign a significant number of points to the portfolio—generally 350 out of a total of 500 for the course—in order to further emphasize its importance. I do not have a rubric with points assigned to each folder within the portfolio because I feel that places a formulaic type of assessment strategy onto something that does not follow a formula, but rather is intended to illustrate the development of a student's writing. However, students are told and given class time to ensure that all aspects of the portfolio are included and complete. This is especially important for the daybook section of the portfolio. As stated earlier, students often do not see or believe in the purpose of maintaining a place that stores all of one's messy thinking; they often have placed value only on their final writing assignments. However, my goal is to show them how the daybook has been the foundation for all the thinking and writing they have done throughout the class—whether informally or formally. Therefore, the daybook section of their portfolio provides them with the chance to return to those seemingly messy and useless writing moments and reflect on the thinking and growing they have done. Here's how my students organize and reflect on their daybook entries.

Daybook Entries

While I would love to look through every page of every student's daybook, this is simply impossible to do given time constraints. Instead of having students turn in their entire daybook, I ask them to copy pages that they feel best illustrate certain moments of development throughout the semester, very similar to Lil's *time for reflection*. (See Figures 7–3 through 7–9.)

Teachers will need to take class time to explain, for example, what exactly a "questioner" daybook entry might look like or include. In Figure 7–3, note how the student specifically states *what* she is questioning in the entry (a piece of text we read in class) and how that questioning is affecting her thinking about the subject (the connection between theory and practice). Students will often want

INSTRUCTIONS FOR *FOLDER 1:* DAYBOOK ENTRIES AND IN-CLASS WRITING

Throughout the semester, you have been asked to write both in class and out of class and to collect that writing in your daybook. You should now collect that work in this folder of your portfolio by selecting and photocopying entries from your daybook. You will copy *two entries* that demonstrate who you have been in this class as *two* of the following:

- a questioner

- a creative thinker

- an analytic thinker

- a collaborator

In order to reflect on the entries you copy, on a sticky note explain how these entries demonstrate those qualities. For instance, you might choose two entries that demonstrate moments of writing where you were a *questioner*. Photocopy those entries, put them in the portfolio, and write a brief explanation on a sticky note for each entry of how this illustrates you as a questioner. Repeat the same process for another quality, like a *collaborator*. This equals four entries total with four sticky note explanations, one on each entry.

You will also

- Look back through your daybook and copy *two moments* of learning that stand out for you. Describe each moment on a sticky note attached to the entry.

- Copy *one entry* where you have written something that you particularly liked. Explain that entry on a sticky note.

Overall, *Folder 1* will have seven daybook entries in it with one sticky note explanation note attached to each entry.

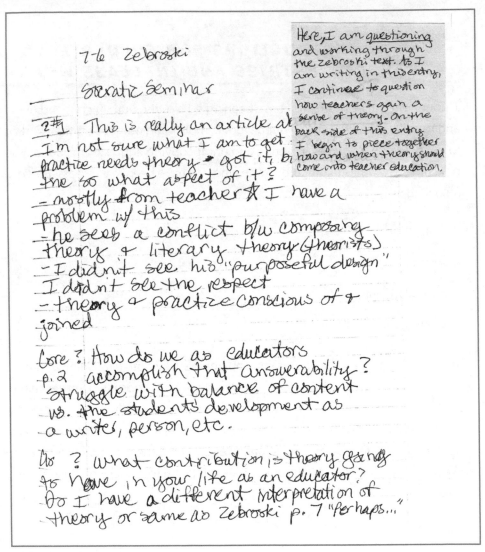

Figure 7–3 *A questioner daybook entry in one student's portfolio.*

to simply label the entry versus describing and reflecting what exactly is happening on that particular page of their daybook. Though there is not one right way to complete this assignment, it is in these flexible moments where further instruction, discussion, and examples can provide students with a truly memorable reflective writing experience. I have found that students enjoy going back and seeing where they have come from and how they got to where they are at the end of the semester as writers as well as questioners, creative and analytic thinkers, and collaborators. I love watching them pore over their daybooks and

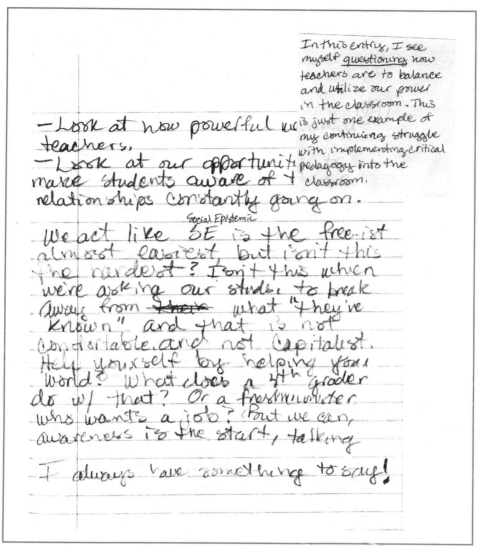

In this entry, I see myself *questioning* how teachers are to balance and utilize our power in the classroom. This is just one example of my continuing struggle with implementing critical pedagogy into the classroom.

— Look at how powerful we teachers.
— Look at our opportunity to make students aware of the relationships constantly going on.

Social Epistemic

We act like SE is the free-ist almost easiest, but isn't this the hardest? Isn't this when we're asking our stud. to break away from ~~their~~ what "they've known" and that is not comfortable, and not Capitalist. Help yourself by helping your world? What does a 4th grader do w/ that? Or a freshman writer who wants a job? But we can, awareness is the start, talking

I always have something to say!

Figure 7–4 *A questioner daybook entry in one student's portfolio.*

have in-depth conversations with each other asking, "Yeah, but which entry *really* shows that I was learning?" That's when I know that something important has happened in our class and the students are learning.

Though I have experienced success with the portfolio, I would caution other teachers to learn from my mistakes. The portfolio takes careful planning and time, and the use of the daybook must be a part of that planning. As I learned the hard way, portfolios are not something that can just be thrown in at the end of the semester. Teachers must have a clear purpose for assessing the daybook via

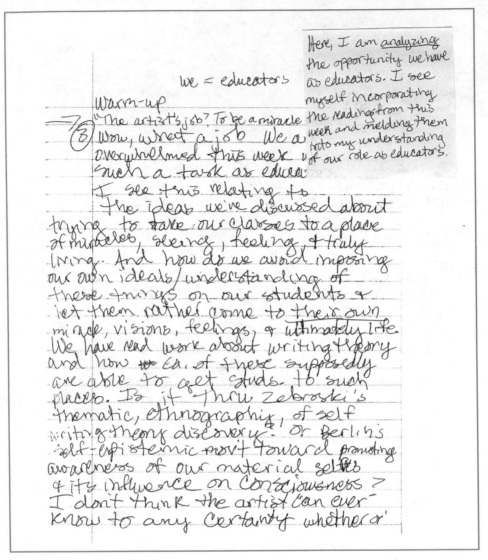

Figure 7–5 *An analytical thinker daybook entry in one student's portfolio.*

a final portfolio. And just as it takes constant kneading and tending to sustain the daybook in a class, assessing the daybook should also be something that has been well thought out and more than a three-ring notebook or folder full of random bits of paper and writing with no connection or reflective thought. I have not only learned that using the daybook to capture students' thinking and writing is a wonderful tool for my class, but I've learned that effectively assessing them produces amazing results.

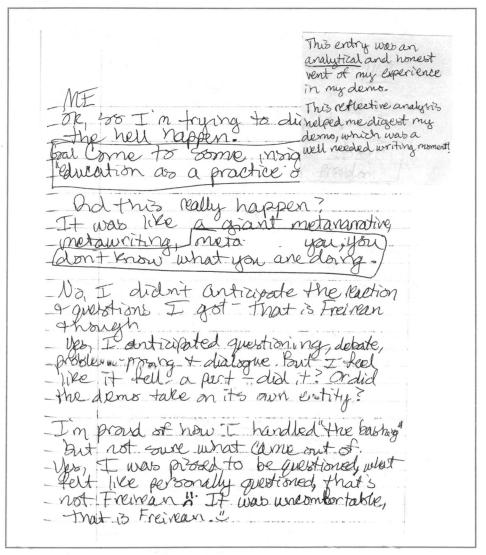

Figure 7–6 *An analytical thinker daybook entry in one student's portfolio.*

Sally's Warning About Assessment and a Strategy for a Nonassessment Assessment

I think it is important to say that teachers do not have to collect or assess the students' daybooks. I don't collect them for many reasons. One is the sheer factor of time and paper—my class load is one hundred or more students and that's too many daybooks for me to assess with the other required work. However, I also

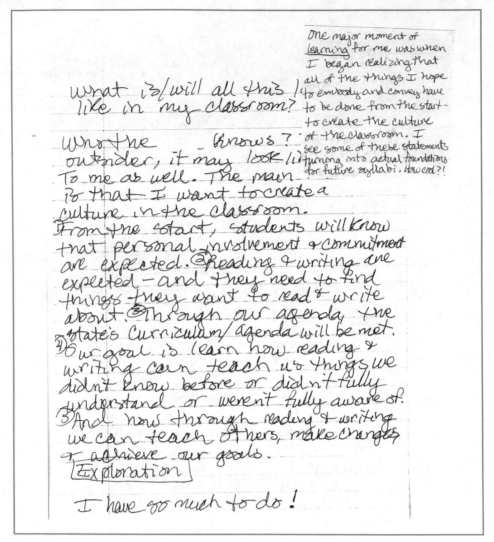

Figure 7–7   *A learning moment daybook entry in one student's portfolio.*

want the students to have a place where they can write anything they want and feel safe that no one will read it, and this brings in trust issues. In order to build trust, some teachers ask students to fold over any pieces of writing that they feel are too personal to share with others. Suppose a teacher does read it? The same trust issue is there when teachers simply ask students to put sticky notes on pages they (teachers) are supposed to read. Suppose the teacher reads something else besides those pages, accidentally or on purpose. These ethical issues are another reason why I don't collect or assess my students' daybooks.

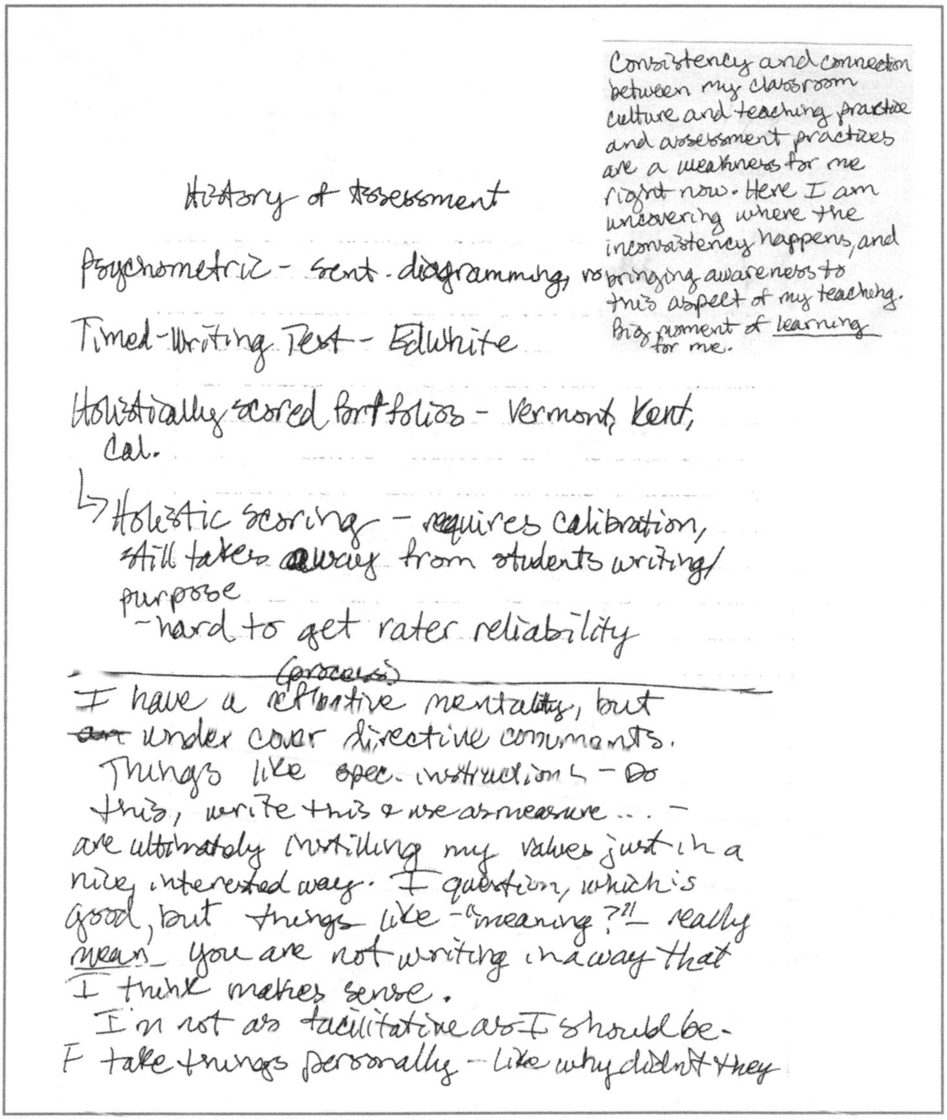

History of Assessment

Psychometric – sent. diagramming, re

Timed-Writing Test – Ed White

Holistically scored Portfolios – Vermont, Kent, Cal.

↳ Holistic scoring – requires calibration, still takes away from students writing/purpose
   – hard to get rater reliability

(process)

I have a reflective mentality, but under cover directive comments. Things like spec. instructions – Do this, write this & use as measure… – are ultimately instilling my values just in a nice, interested way. I question, which is good, but things like – "meaning?" really mean you are not writing in a way that I think makes sense.
   I'm not as facilitative as I should be. I take things personally – like why didn't they

Consistency and connection between my classroom culture and teaching practice and assessment practices are a weakness for me right now. Here I am uncovering where the inconsistency happens, and bringing awareness to this aspect of my teaching. Big moment of learning for me.

Figure 7–8   *A learning moment daybook entry in one student's portfolio.*

So like Karen's quick assessments, I always try to find ways to informally notice what my students are doing. For example, if I ask my students to write their first drafts in their daybooks, when they get into their listening friends circle I look over their shoulders to see that they are indeed reading from a draft. I give students a completion grade for sharing their draft, and I have not compromised the writing in their daybooks. Any time I check anything in their daybook, I ask students to turn to that page and show me that piece *only*. I usually don't read

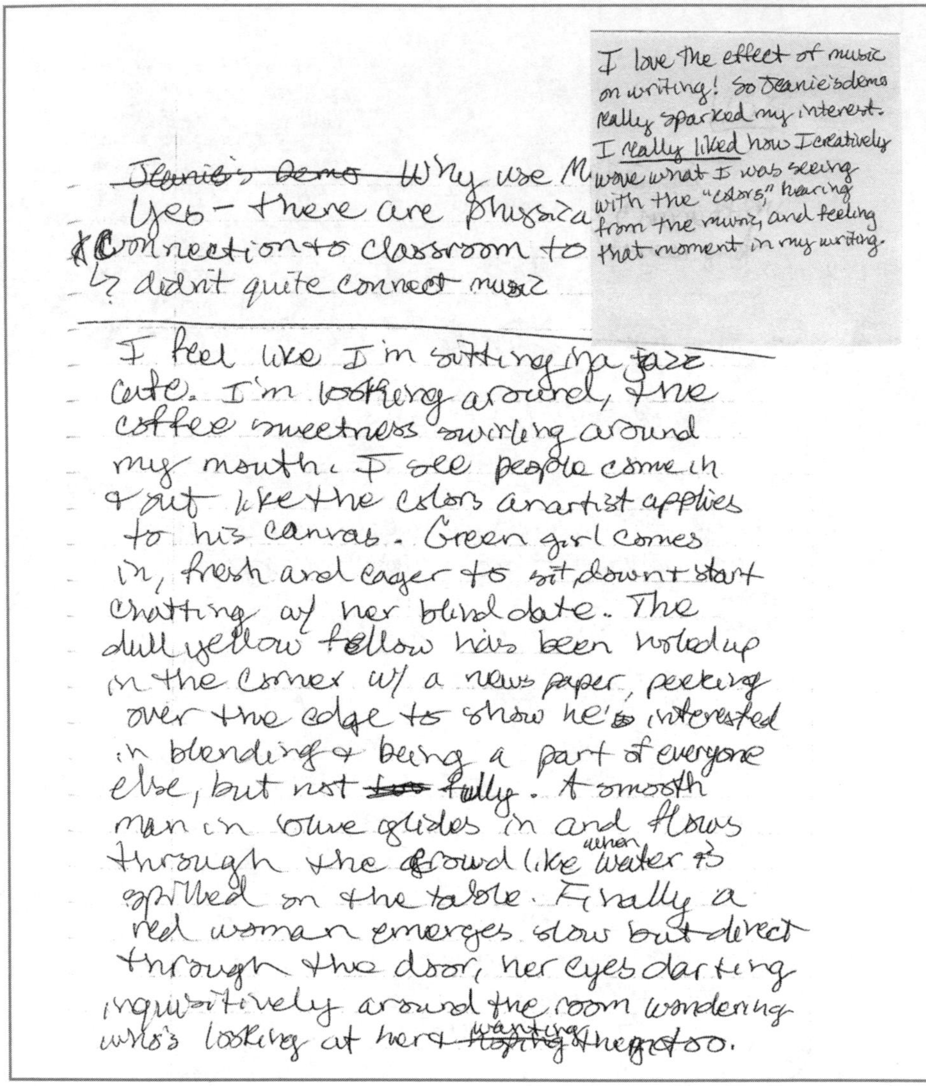

I love the effect of music on writing! So Jeanie's demo really sparked my interest. I really liked how I creatively wove what I was seeing with the "colors," hearing from the music, and feeling that moment in my writing.

~~Jeanie's Demo~~ Why use M...
Yes – there are physica...
Connection to classroom to...
↳ didn't quite connect music

I feel like I'm sitting in a jazz cafe. I'm looking around, the coffee sweetness swirling around my mouth. I see people come in & out like the colors an artist applies to his canvas. Green girl comes in, fresh and eager to sit down & start chatting w/ her blind date. The dull yellow fellow has been holed up in the corner w/ a newspaper, peeking over the edge to show he's interested in blending & being a part of everyone else, but not ~~too~~ fully. A smooth man in blue glides in and flows through the crowd like water when is spilled on the table. Finally a red woman emerges slow but direct through the door, her eyes darting inquisitively around the room wondering who's looking at her & ~~hoping~~ wanting them too.

Figure 7–9 *An entry I liked daybook entry in one student's portfolio.*

from their daybooks just check to see if the work is there. They draw from the daybooks to write their final papers, which I do read.

Concluding Thoughts

Whether teachers informally or formally assess daybooks, students are responsible for selecting out their work, analyzing it, and reflecting on how it represents them as writers and thinkers. In the end, assessment issues we have fought in the past—only caring about the *A*, writing for the teacher, and assignments that don't connect—are eliminated when we use daybooks to capture student thinking and learning. Once our students realize that it's not the grade that matters but their growth as writers, an invisible weight is lifted and we can get down to the real purpose of our classes—becoming better thinkers. The daybook has captured that growth in a magically messy way.

What to Remember About Assessment

Having students become investigators of their writing is clearly what matters. The more students become reflective, the more students will be learning.

- Have a clear purpose for using daybooks.

- Have students select what is to be checked or reflected upon.

- Have students write much more in their daybooks than a teacher will actually read or evaluate.

- Have students focus on their own growth and development as writers and thinkers through daybook reflections.

Using Daybooks in Teacher Research

Basic research is what I'm doing when I don't know what I'm doing.

—Wernher von Braun

In those opening minutes of class when students are reflecting on their lives and exploring ideas in their daybooks, we too, have important daybook work to do. It is important for us to write whenever our students are writing, to model for them our struggles and triumphs as writers. But we also know that after lunch, or when third period comes into the classroom, or at the end of the day, when we are modeled out the personal reflection writing just isn't as spontaneous as it was earlier in the day. The moments when we are writing with our students or quietly for ourselves are the ones we use for researching our practices, for writing to reflect on our teaching, and to be teacher researchers. *Teacher re-*

searcher is not a fancy title only a few of us have. It is a title that we claim when we reflect on our teaching.

Who Has Time to Reflect?

There are a variety of good excuses for not writing, but mostly we all seem to wonder what happened to that time we thought we would have each day to think and reflect. With department meetings and hall duty, parents' questions and after-school detention, teachers don't have a chance to think, much less write. The daybook, however, gives us the place to jot down our thoughts in those brief moments that we have during the day, and it allows us to collect our thoughts over time. Each of us works in similar ways, so in this chapter when Karen writes about her elementary classroom, what she does there is similar to what Shana and Lil do in their college classes. When Cindy and Sally talk about their work in high school classrooms, Tony and Karen have done similar things in their elementary schools as well. We trust that their stories will resonate with teachers of all grade levels, to all teachers who want to think about teaching and learning. These teachers, and indeed all teachers who consider how to improve their classroom, are teacher researchers.

The Daybook: A Place for Teachers to Record Experience and Change Practice

Ann Berthoff (1981) , Dixie Goswami and Peter Stillman (1986), and James Britton (1982) have all made important arguments for the power and usefulness of teacher narrative reflection on the classroom. Our work in this book is a testament to the importance of teachers recording their experiences and changing their practices in light of their work with students. Cy Knoblauch and Lil Brannon (1988) give us a way of understanding the importance of story, reminding us that story "(from the Latin *historia*) is a form of narrative, a verbal memory of human experience, a record—a telling—of what life is like" (23). Stories are told by someone to someone for a reason. They are composed and interpreted.

The teacher researcher's story is important because the teacher is the insider, the narrator. "The narrator inhabits the world of the classroom, knows it from the inside, does not 'descend' upon it for a short time, edit out what has been judged irrelevant in advance, and test its observations against general hypotheses that have been formulated without reference to it. The telling aims not at selectivity or simplification [like empirical investigation] but at richness of texture and intentional complexity. The telling does not seek to highlight problems and solutions, or causes and effects, or stimuli and responses, or rights and wrongs, or heroes or villains, but seeks instead to depict, to evoke … the 'life world'—that palpable, sensual, kaleidoscopic, mysterious reality that constitutes our material rather than merely intellectual existence" (1988, 24–25).

Karen's Story: Keeping Track of Learning

At first my daybook was just a tool to write down the gist of the lessons I taught, the students' reactions to them, and my ideas for making the lessons better. I still do that, but now I write for my own learning and to keep track of everything that goes on in more detail. I collect these kernels and turn them into articles about teaching.

For instance, once when I was conferencing individually with children for weeks, I came across a young writer whose story was quite good, but her spelling was poor. I asked her how she checked her story. She shared a frustrating tale of writing, checking, and thinking her spelling was correct. Even the next day, she was distressed by the spelling mistakes she had missed.

I suggested that when she finished her text and had read it over several times to make sure the story made sense, she turn her paper over and sit for about five minutes. She could even draw on her scrap paper to take her mind off her story. Then I told her to start reading her paper from the end. Read the last word first and then the second to last word. "Read your story as if it is a list of words," I told her. "That way you will be reading just to check spelling and your mind won't trick you into thinking you wrote every word right." She looked at me blankly. I told her to try it. Her last line was, "Then he gave it to me."

She started reading: "eeemmm, ooottt, tiii."

I wrote in my daybook, "Make sure students understand not to read the words backwards when you explain this editing suggestion." By writing down what happened, I remember the details of the story. The simple act of recording keeps the story alive. I use my daybook table of contents to find an anecdote, or a book, a page number, or an idea. The daybook becomes my storage closet, my place to return to discover and reflect on my teaching. It contains the record of this story and the other threads I am now weaving into the tapestry of this chapter. The daybook is my place for drafting the meat and potatoes of my writing. Teacher research can be as simple as that.

▶ Students as Coinvestigators

Once I used my daybook to study revision. I thought that a careful study of my practices would aid me in helping my students make the kinds of changes that would develop their work. I was tired of the one-draft-done approach that many of my students were taking, or their belief that revision was simply a matter of fixing the spelling. When I began this study, I knew I would learn a lot about myself as a teacher. What I had not anticipated was that my research would also affect my students.

A fourth-grade child approached me one day and asked, "I revised this lead. Is it good enough to go in *your* daybook?" At first, I was taken aback. "Why *my* daybook?" He said, "You are always writing cool stuff in your daybook. I want to be in there, too." I immediately wrote his sentence in my daybook. He as well as all of my students saw that when they did something I found worth writing down, I usually said something like, "Wow. I really liked how you reorganized that paragraph. Do you mind if I copy that in my daybook?" This observant child believed that if I recorded his lead in my daybook, he had written well. To him, it was better than an *A*. The teacher wanted to record his writing forever. I still remember his lead to this day: "I don't really believe this story, but my mom says it's true." I know because I have a record of his writing in my daybook.

Sally's Story: Reaching Hard-to-Reach Students

The twelve sixth graders tumbled into my classroom in mid-August—chattering to each other, sticky from running outside in the near 90 degree heat—and scattered themselves in various seats and positions throughout my classroom. The students had been rejected as not prepared or ineligible for electives taught during this period in our junior high/middle school. It was a transition year for us; We were switching from the junior high to the middle school concept, a move that crowded grades six through nine in one school and turned our campus into a trailer park. To make matters more difficult, we were adopting block scheduling for the high schools, which now included the ninth graders, but not the sixth, seventh, or eighth graders.

The twelve children in my hot August classroom had been plucked early from their elementary schools and plopped into the middle of a bell-ringing disaster. Amid their confusion, their behavior had not been the best, which banned them from the traditional electives—art, chorus, shop, computer training, cooking. I had volunteered, as a ninth-grade English and creative writing teacher, to find something for these children to do. In conversation it seemed like a novel idea and a challenge, but as their chattering continued throughout roll call and an introduction to the class, I wondered how anything that initially appeared so simple could suddenly have turned threatening. By the end of the forty-five-minute period, I was exhausted. I sat down at my desk just to catch my breath and try to gain some composure during the last half of my planning period. What would I do with this dirty dozen?

At the time I did not know that these kids would open up a new world for me—a daybook in which I examined methods to reach them, their personalities and how they fit into our school, and my views on teaching and children. My day-book, the same one I had used for so long to write with my students and occasionally to record ideas to use or more things to think about, was about to become an ethnography—a chronicle of my journey through theories and ideologies to an understanding of myself and my students—and a compost pile of simmering ideas and questions. Ralph Fletcher (1996) speaks of the writer's notebook as a compost pile. He sees writing in his notebook as having four different potentials: transformation (the simmering for change), fertility, randomness, and wait time (59). My compost for this class was becoming rich in randomness, but I didn't have time to let it simmer. I had to have a workable idea by 7:15 the next morning.

The six-week summer stint soon stretched throughout the entire school year because the principal began to see that these so-called problem students were learning. I used my daybook to plan lessons for them. Boy, did I plan lessons. Sometimes it was a lesson for the entire class. Other times, it became a study of one child and lists of ideas to try to reach him.

▶ Sally and Anthony

Anthony lived with his grandmother and had issues with authority, which manifested itself as a refusal to do anything he was directed to do. I wrote in my daybook:

> I have to reach Anthony or he will sit in that chair and do nothing for the whole semester. I have tried sitting near him during freewrites to model behavior and that didn't work. I have demanded that he do it and that was a disaster. He needs to think that he thought it up himself. If it is his idea, it isn't a problem. Perhaps if I listed some topics on the board before freewrite Anthony would choose one. Maybe if I talked to Anthony and found something that he really is interested in, I could add something similar to the list and that would get him started.

My first attempt did not work, but I continued my conversation with Anthony. Eventually he helped me to find where his interests lay, and he started writing. By the end of the first marking period, Anthony was producing poetry focused on his family, particularly on his mother, who he felt had abandoned him. I found some of Paul Lawrence Dunbar's poems about children and we wrote poems like Dunbar's. Anthony couldn't stop writing poems. As he wrote and I read what he wrote, we talked about my children. Anthony was quick to give me advice on how I could better communicate with my son and daughters. I recorded Anthony's suggestions and chronicled his progress. His daybook bulged with freewrites and with pieces he had clipped and pasted; some were Dunbar's.

When it came time to publish, Anthony spent hours poring over his daybook to choose the pieces that he felt best reflected who he was.

▶ Sally and Mary Ann

Mary Ann presented a different problem. She wrote all the time—in her daybook, to her friends, in the margins of books, but she wouldn't share any of her writing and she wouldn't talk. Conversations with Mary Ann revealed a household dominated by an older father whose rule was that children should be seen and not heard. "He did not see how a child could add anything to the conversation," Mary Ann said. Rather, the child should be always listening and watching to learn the right way to communicate. I wrote:

> I want Mary Ann to have a good experience at school, and I certainly want her to share with the others. Because she is so silent and watchful, the details in her writing are outstanding. She never misses anything and she is adept at finding the right metaphor or simile. How can I get her to show the others the virtue of watching and listening and at the same time get them to help her learn the enjoyment of sharing?

> Through my observations of Mary Ann when she talked as well as through my conversations with her, when she was silent, I learned how to offer praise of specific pieces and to encourage other students to do the same until Mary Ann became comfortable reading her work aloud and offering her opinion on the work of others. She became a valuable resource for them.

Although many of the entries in my daybook that year were for immediate thinking and use—no time for waiting, immediate action needed—they did take on the semblance of compost later when I reviewed them for ideas for helping my next students. The notes I had written about Anthony, Mary Ann, and the others formed rich nuggets that grew into lessons, units, and eventually a whole new way of teaching. The dirty dozen's problems were the same as those of other children.

▶ Learning About Yourself as a Teacher

In writing as a teacher researcher, you learn as much about yourself as about the person or group that you study. I certainly continue to learn about myself and about my school culture. I wrote in my daybook:

> It seems that the children who need the most from school get the least. Somehow they get lost in the shuffle as we struggle to do the bidding of the influential parents.

My ideas about education that year took a 180 degree turn. I interviewed children, transcribed the interviews, and pasted them into my daybook. I marked similarities and differences. I looked for traits along the lines of race, class, gender, and culture. I read the students' work beside the students' interviews and looked for clues to help me help them with their writing. I became interested in the relationship between student reading and student writing and kept double- (and sometimes) triple-entry pages on what I found. All of this festered in my mind, and I explored the ideas in my daybook alongside my daily musings with the students and my after-class assessments of each day's classes (my lessons, their performance).

▶ *Sally and Ronnie*

I took my daybook with me when the ninth grade relocated to the high school in the fall. One student, Ronnie, posed a new set of problems. He saw himself as a writer. He wrote, but he never finished the pieces, and he never handed in anything he wrote. I would watch him start writing a piece, listen to him read portions to his group, but a search through the papers rarely yielded one with his name on it. Ronnie's reading was more sporadic than his writing. On days when we sat in a circle and shared golden lines from our reading, Ronnie never shared from the same book twice. He also never finished a book—the first three chapters were as far as he ever got. Audiotaped and transcribed conversations with Ronnie at first gave me little to go on. He was easily bored with reading books, he would say. Then he would say he loved reading. I asked questions to probe his past reading habits. His sister used to read to him, but she had moved out and now no one in his house wanted to read or talk about reading. He played videogames and watched television with his stepfather. I turned to notes I had made in a previous daybook when I struggled with another writer whose problems seemed similar to Ronnie's. I photocopied the pages and pasted them into my current daybook near the interviews with Ronnie. I searched another daybook for lessons I might use. If the lessons worked another time, surely they might work for Ronnie. My prewriting lessons on generating ideas seemed to engage Ronnie, and I recorded his reactions in my daybook. But Ronnie did not seem to respond to my never-fail tried-and-true daily activities. I wondered if he was just getting older and more jaded. The old prods that teachers had used on him no longer worked. He needed new stimuli to make him feel that what he had to say was worth as much as the other students. Ronnie's difficulties as a writer intrigued me and became the impetus behind an after-school program I developed for reluctant writers. What happened to Ronnie? Ronnie discovered that he loved poetry.

He graduated from high school, and the last time I spoke with him, he told me that he kept a small notebook with him at work where he wrote down ideas that he would use in poems later.

▶ Why Daybooks for Teachers

The daybooks are as valuable to me as the books by the gurus in the writing profession. The gurus have given me the tools, but the experience of using these tools in my own real-life classroom is between the covers of the daybooks. I write to discover what the children are saying to me and what I know about children, this age in general and these in particular. I write in my daybook every day immediately after school. Some days that time stretches to twenty minutes; some days it shrinks to five. But every day I have some notation about the effect of my ideas on the children's learning. My book of ideas is growing and so is my storehouse of research. I have much more than lesson plans. I have profiles and reflections that I can use to improve my teaching. My daybook has helped me learn about my students, myself, lessons, the school culture, and my role in the lives of these students. I have learned, and I have learned through writing.

Cindy's Story: Pulling It All Together

My daybook helps me to see my teaching in a whole new way. I was fortunate enough to be a part of a teacher research group led by Sally along with Pat English. They encouraged us to write for fifteen minutes each day about what was happening in our classrooms. Once I began the habit, I never stopped. Sometimes I do my writing during class as my students write. Other times I do it at the end of the day, sitting at my desk with my hot tea and special lamp, trying to get my paper-grading mojo on. Either way, it makes me stop and think about what is happening, or not happening, with my students. Even better, it helps me home in on individual students and puzzle out what is going on with them.

My classroom has become completely workshop-based over the years and I constantly defend my practices to those around me. As I worked with my students and wrote in my daybook, I began to see patterns and ideas form, things that I wanted to say to the rest of the world. I read theory supporting teachers in student-centered classrooms and wrote about that reading in my daybook. I had conversations with other professionals in the field and wrote about them in my daybook. I attended conferences and wrote about them in my daybook. Before long, I had a book in my daybook, or multiple daybooks by this point.

As I sit down to my computer each day to tell the story on my classroom, my daybooks are never far from reach. When I come to a point I want to illustrate but can't remember exactly what I want to use, I go to my daybooks and browse. Something will be there. When I'm in the middle of a piece of writing and run out of time, a note about where I am and where I want to be goes in my daybook, and I work on it in short bursts throughout the day while my students are writing. And then my students almost always do or say something that adds another layer to what I'm writing.

And when I get to the revision stage, I can't function at all without my daybook. My book (Urbanski 2006b) went through massive changes between contract and publication. I read the reviews and sat about the work of revising for a real audience that was quite vocal about what they liked and didn't like. By that time, I was sick of every word of that manuscript, and my daybook helped me to see it all in a new way. When I revise, I often record thoughts in my daybook about where paragraphs should go and what I should do next, almost simultaneously with what I am doing on the computer. I work on one section, and the solution for the chapter I was struggling with last night pops into my head. I jot that down in my daybook and continue with what I'm doing on the computer. At the end of a writing session, I leave notes for myself in my daybook describing what I should do the next time I roll out of bed at 5:00 A.M. and sit in front of my computer with my coffee. That way, I can just dive in and let the words flow—or not—depending on the way the muses are responding to me that day.

▶ The Life of a Piece of Writing

In looking through old daybooks for examples for this chapter, I discovered something. The kernels of the daybook defense (see Chapter 7) and what I would eventually come to write about it existed in places I had forgotten. I was not surprised to find a draft of the letter I wrote to my students upon discovering their cheating, nor was I shocked to see pasted in copies of letters from students begging for the reinstatement of the daybook. What's interesting is that I wrote no reflection with these pieces, and my writing that follows deals with another project that I was working on and completely ignores those pieces and the events that inspired them. In my memory, that was the end of writing about the daybook until over a year later when I suddenly began to write about it again.

But when I look back, I see a series of clusters and writing in my daybook that I did with my students just a couple of months later. The point of the activity was to introduce another tool for discovering writing topics. I introduced it to each of my three classes so I wrote three times in one day. (See Figures 8–1a, 8–1b.)

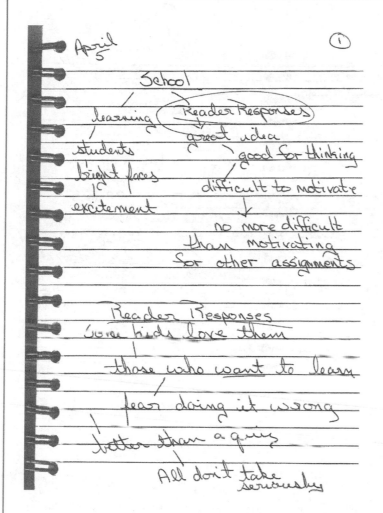

Golub [I had recently heard Jeffrey Golub speak at a conference] summed up what it's all about for me last week. I shouldn't be focused on preparing students for the next teacher, the next class, or the next test. I should be focused on helping students be better readers, thinkers, and writers by the end of the year.

I had forgotten that! So what if the teachers they have next year give reading quizzes or multiple choice, in-class tests instead of portfolios? So what if L. doesn't give tests at all? *So what* if students are complaining that my class is more work? I think I started questioning whether or not it was all too much.

So . . . how can I make these R.R. more effective without turning it into a policing thing?

Concept #1 teaching in any American school is that students need to be "paid" to work. Sure, there are some bright and shining lights who want to learn for the sake of learning, but let's be real here . . . who's really going to do it? So we need *grades*. Truly, I think I got lazy about spot-checking responses and not allowing students with no responses to work in the groups—therefore, some of them never saw the value of the assignment because they were never forced to do it.

I've also had way too many kids who simply do not bring their daybooks to class. Then there was the *Les Mis* fiasco. I let the cheaters get to me. I took it personally that they weren't reading and went into Nazi police mode. I'd been struggling with community building this year and that incident completely derailed it. We completely lost our workshop environment and, as several students pointed out, I became just like any other English teacher.

Figure 8–1a *Excerpts from a teacher researcher's daybook.*

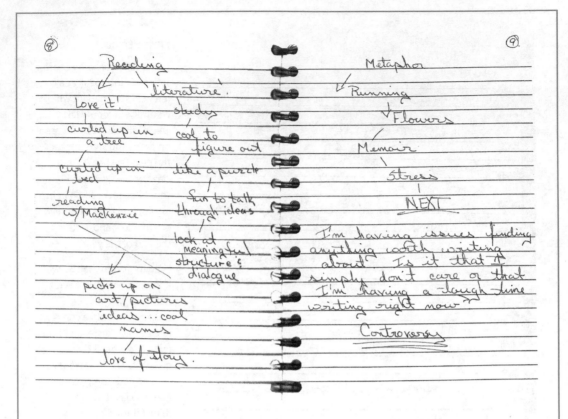

SECOND PERIOD

I'm having issues finding anything worth writing about. Is it that I simply don't care or that I'm having a tough time writing right now?

How *awesome*!

This stuff works! Bret and Phillip of all people are in heated discussion about what to write about—he just said, "You can take this idea anywhere."

Crap! This is all fine and dandy but I still don't want to write about it! The writing today has been good in terms of helping me figure out where things went wrong, but an essay or piece of writing about it simply feels whiny and tedious … like all of my writing for the past six months … and I am *so* tired of whiny and tedious. What I need to do is stop futzing around and get back into a writing habit like I *know* I need in order to have anything good.

So … I still have to have something for the teacher research group. What about what happens when writing/reading workshop goes wrong … a story of intrigue and mystery. That could be my metaphor!

It was a beautiful late summer day and I had something to prove! I knew everything.

Figure 8—1b *Excerpts from a teacher researcher's daybook.*

It seems as though I have almost hit my gear at the end of this entry, but I didn't. Flipping through my daybook, I find that my frustration with what to write about continued for several months. Just a few pages later, I've switched to fiction and am struggling with that too. There's even a page about two weeks after the entries you've seen here that holds the beginnings of an essay and application for a Ph.D. program. I was so frustrated with myself as a teacher that I was seriously thinking about escaping it all by going back to school—a good idea, but for the wrong reasons.

The most interesting thing to me about all of this is that I forgot about it completely. I remember it now, looking back through these pages, but I also know how the story ends. I spent the summer at Bard and then teaching the UNC Charlotte Writing Project Summer Institute. Through all of the writing and thinking about teaching I did there, I came up with the idea of the daybook defense that we've already discussed in Chapter 7. A year and one month from the first set of entries you've seen, I spoke with Tom Romano about the daybook defense in a session and he asked me if I had written an article about it. The answer was of course no, but his words were the kick in the pants I needed. I chronicled what happened after I spoke with Tom Romano in my daybook. (See Figure 8–2.)

This goes on for four pages and then has a note at the bottom, "see page 141," where it goes on for five more pages. I began drafting the daybook defense article in earnest as soon as school ended; it was first published as a journal article (Urbanski 2006a) and then it was rewritten for this book.

When I was writing the article, I forgot about my struggles a year earlier to write about my classroom. I forgot my fear that after completing *Using the Workshop Approach* (Urbanski 2006b), I'd never be able to write anything good again. But looking back, I know that I needed to do that writing. I had to figure out what was going on with me as well as with my students. I'm also glad to have my daybook entries, so that I can remember the humbling experience of that year. Those kids and I get along famously now. After our second year together, I chaperoned twenty-five of them on a trip to Europe, and half of them were the original cause of my frustration. I am reminded of the payoff of sticking to my academic guns by the fact that last week their senior English teacher emailed to say that they had "rocked" their IB Oral Exams with the most independent, individual, thoughtful analysis of passages she had ever heard. This was from the kids who wanted to copy reader responses from Cliff's Notes as sophomores!

▶ The Effect on My Students

My students, like Karen's and Sally's, know that I am a writer. They are always aware of where I am in the process. They commiserated with me over each

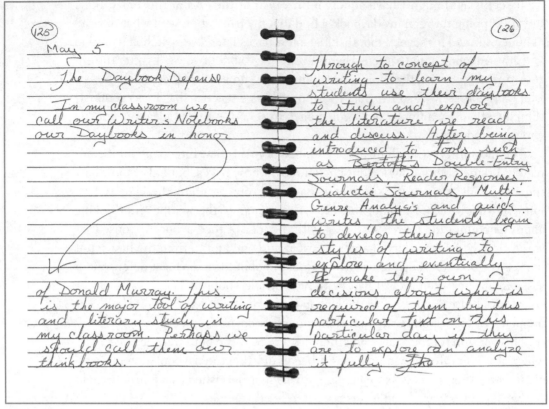

Figure 8–2 *A daybook entry about writing a new book.*

rejection and they celebrated with me when I received a book contract. When I hit the wall, they remind me of my own advice for breaking through it. When they discover something new about writing, they share it with me as I do with them. And when they have difficulty with their writing, they trust me because they've seen me go through those same struggles.

Because I'm always writing, I know that sometimes a writer needs bald honesty about the piece and sometimes she needs to have her ego stroked, to have someone point out and focus on the one golden line or idea in the pile of useless words. I know that sometimes a writer needs someone else to say, "This just isn't working" or "This is working, but I need to know more about. . . ." Because I write, I know that writing can't happen in a vacuum. I know that we need other people to read our writing.

Because I am a writer, my students see the daybook modeled in the real world as a tool for writing as well as thinking about writing and reading. They trust it because they see it work for me. They know that the daybook's uses, forms, and organization are ever-changing because they see that in action. And as I write about my students and our classroom each day, I find more and more stories to tell. But I don't have to worry about them slipping away because they are all right there in my daybook, waiting for their 5:00 A.M. appointment.

Daybooks as Instruments for Change

Teachers, no matter what grade level they teach, know more about what happens in the classroom than anyone else. Yet when it comes to educational policy and to the curriculum, teachers are often the last ones consulted, if they are consulted at all. In fact, more often than not, teachers are told what to do, given pacing guides and, in our area, scripted lessons to teach and then blamed when students do badly. Through teacher research, teachers can claim their voices and document what happens in their classrooms. When we are teacher-researchers, we deviate from the script, not because we are being belligerent or because we think we are smarter than the folks who wrote it, but because we are the ones in our classrooms and with our students each day. We are the ones who see where they are and what they need. Our daybooks help us document and think about all that is happening in our classrooms and adapt to what our students need in order to learn based on that information.

Reflecting on our thinking about teaching makes our classrooms exciting places to be. We can look carefully at who we are and what we do. We can think about our interactions with our students, their histories, their struggles, their successes, and we can make our teaching better. Our daybook captures the *better* that we find in our classrooms. For the inquiring principal or curious parent, our daybooks are our documentation of why we do what we do. We find it hard for anyone to question our practices when we have evidence of our observations made during our lessons of what didn't work, our notes from reading, our researched ideas on what to do differently, and our reflections and student samples of how the implementation of those ideas improved learning. That is why our daybooks matter more than we can say.

What to Remember About Daybooks and Teacher Research

Daybooks can become your way of keeping track of your teaching life. Unlike the lesson-plan book that you have to turn in to the principal or keep in case there is a substitute teacher, your daybook can record what you actually did in your classroom and what you really thought about it. Your daybook is your thinking, and you will treasure it and return to it.

- Model, model, model, model, model.

- When you start writing, everything you ever felt, believed, or understood about teaching will come tumbling out.

- Your organizing system—your table of contents, sticky notes, what have you—will help you find your stories when you go to write.

- On those days when the loudspeaker comes on just as you come to the most important line in the poem, when the heat doesn't work in your "learning cottage," when there is a random assembly that conflicts with this great lesson that you planned, open your daybook and read your stories and be reminded of why you are a teacher.

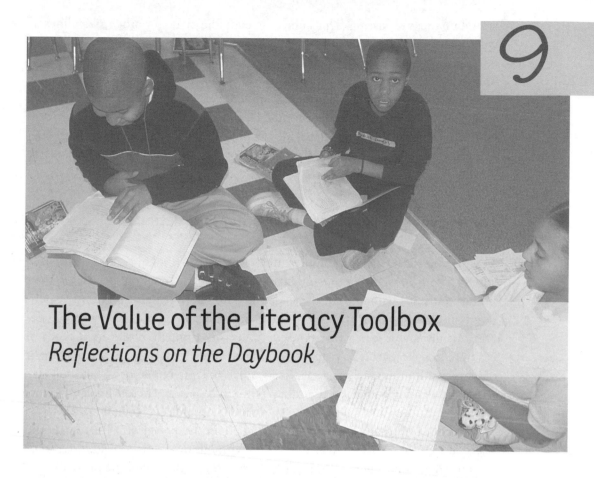

The Value of the Literacy Toolbox
Reflections on the Daybook

We now accept the fact that learning is a lifelong process of keeping abreast of change. And the most pressing task is to teach people how to learn.

—PETER F. DRUCKER

In order to empower children, we must help them think critically about the world around them. Literacy practices like daybook reflections can morph into critical thinking. As teachers we need to help children build a toolbox that can take them anywhere they may have to or want to go. Yet, to teachers who haven't used them, daybooks can seem like a lot of work. Ask teachers who are familiar with the daybook and they'll tell you it is worth the effort.

However, implementing anything new that isn't a worksheet or something with an exact step-by-step plan can seem messy. Teaching and learning the five-paragraph theme is far easier than teaching and learning the nuts and bolts and subtle nuances of writing. The same case could be made for other disciplines as well. Cookbook labs in science are much easier than real experiments; following one right way to do a math equation is easier than understanding the logic that mathematicians use to solve a problem; studying history and social sciences solely from a textbook by memorizing facts and dates is simpler than discovering the contested nature of so-called historical facts. The concern with formulaic academic methods is that they offer students only one way to do things—the school way. Education becomes an exercise in memorizing and regurgitating rather than thinking, analyzing, and problem solving.

The Daybook's Importance in Literacy Instruction

The daybook is a tool that promotes literacy as critical thinking and complex reasoning. It provides a place for students to think and try things out, to stretch their literary muscles without fear of academic alienation. It helps students experiment and find the best writing and the best organization for a given writing situation. It gives students a variety of ways to work through all different types of reading. It gives teachers a place to record and study what they are seeing in their classrooms. It gives teachers a space to write in order to remember what their students are dealing with each time they put pen to paper. The daybook can even go digital. But daybooks need to be there in classrooms everywhere, every day.

In light of all that we have been saying about the power of reflection in the daybook, we thought it only fitting to end with our own reflections on our journeys to create multiliterate, versatile writers through the use of the daybook. We offer our stories to those who are experimenting with daybooks for the first time as well to those who have been using them for a while but are hitting roadblocks or feeling frustrated. We've all been there and have found that talking with one another and sharing our stories has helped us remember why we were going through the process in the first place. We begin with Shana's reflection on how she made the connection between theory and practice.

Shana's Story: Critical Theory Meets Practice

When my students walk into my room on the first day, I tell them that one of my main goals is to help them develop as writers and, more importantly, as active and critical thinkers. I want to help them become critically conscious of the world they live in and provide them with a place to read, write, and discuss that world. Though I always knew that I wanted to create change within my students, my

The Daybook: A Way to Redefine Our Literacy Instruction

The Potential Value of the Language of Home

James Britton and his colleagues at the London Schools Council Project (1975) demonstrated the importance of students using expressive language, the language of the home, as the voice they use in when writing in their daybooks. The language closest to the self/home is the language that all of us think in. Writing informally in daybooks brings children's home language into the school and with it their life experiences, values, and ideas.

The Potential Harm of School Literacy

Deborah Brandt (1998) shows how "school literacy" can actually be harmful. Traditional education can cripple students by requiring them to spend months of their time doing formulaic writing activities from the five-paragraph theme to the tried-and-true, no-fail AP or SAT essay. Months spent on these assembly lines—even when they are taken through a hobbled writing process (first draft, slot ideas into three paragraphs, correct)—gives students very limited views of how writing works and narrows their thinking to quick solutions that have three reasons. When the world changes as rapidly as it does in the twenty-first century, a person needs to have complex literacy practices, which means the ability to think critically and argue cogently to audiences very unlike themselves in cultures whose values differ from their own. Students need practice in thinking deeply, seeing alternative views, researching their experiences and their lives, and writing in many genres for many purposes. In other words, they need ways of making their voices heard in new and even unpredictable situations.

We shortchange our students when we present them with singular modes and forms of literacy. What happens when the formula a teacher drilled in school no longer applies to the world the student comes to live in as an adult? Brandt contends that it means that a worker is no longer needed in a position that was at one time her livelihood. In North Carolina, where we live, we are seeing that when the mills close, entire communities are jobless and lack the skills they need to pursue an alternate career. We also see that when the banks outsource their accounting to another country, young workers struggle to find new ways to make a living. All of these more global issues can be traced back to literacy development in the classroom. Therefore, as literacy teachers, we must consider how we are or are not preparing our students to be effective, literate citizens.

Redefining Literacy

Certainly we can't expect teachers to predict what the literacy needs will be in the next fifteen years—that would be a waste of time and energy. Instead, we should extend our energy to foster adaptive literacy in students and challenge their literacy at every turn so that they find a comfort level within change and challenge. Our goal is to nurture natural curiosity and questioning, to create a nation of thinkers and give people the power to make and question meaning.

quest toward a more critically conscious classroom didn't come to fruition until I was assigned to read Paulo Freire's *Pedagogy of the Oppressed* (1970) in a graduate literary theory course. As a teaching assistant at the time and teaching three freshman composition courses, as I read the text I was forced to contemplate my philosophies, expectations, and practices as a teacher. After completing the book, I felt compelled to change. I did not realize it exactly at the time, but I started to rethink my classroom and the roles I played within it. I became more aware of what I was doing as a teacher and why I was teaching in certain ways. I wanted my students to be more aware of who they were as thinkers and knowers.

Just as Freire was becoming important in my philosophy as a teacher, I learned about daybooks in another one of my Master's courses and almost instantly saw how useful daybooks would be for me as a student, allowing me to unify my ideas in a messy yet purposeful way. My daybook was the place where I stored all my thinking as both a student learning about Freire and a teacher wanting to implement Freirean pedagogies. Accordingly, while Freire's philosophy became a permanent part of my teaching philosophy, I also immediately began using daybooks in my own first-year composition classrooms in order to provide my students with a tool to makes sense of their thoughts.

As an instructor of first-year composition, which like many other courses is often a place where students are very concerned with being correct, I consistently felt as though my students viewed me as their permanent editor. They were reluctant to share their writing with anyone other than me, their teacher. I had to find a way to work through this issue common in most any writing class.

When I began using daybooks as a student, my pages became filled with things that were relevant to the particular courses I was taking—notes from reading, responses to comments in class, and snippets and drafts for writing assignments. Then, I found myself making connections between the ideas we talked about in my graduate classes and the classes I was teaching. This is when things got interesting. I began thinking about the implications of Friere's critical pedagogy and then questioning my goals in first-year writing. Rather than assigning my students the traditional research paper, I began having my students research the corporate logos that filled our classrooms—the logos on shirts, coffee cups, sneakers, and bulletin boards. Through Freire's notion of critical questioning and problem posing, my students began to wonder about the sweatshop labor that made some products seemingly affordable in the United States, and they began to question corporate policies such as outsourcing that made jobs in our local community scarce (Marklin and Woodward 2006).

Most of my students' critical thinking and researching happened in the their daybooks. Through various minilessons, I showed them all the different ways that my own daybook helped me think and plan. Intrigued, my students began following suit, doing all of their thinking in their daybooks. Because I was writing along with them, the dynamics of the classroom shifted. No longer was I the all-knowing teacher, editor for their writing, holder of the red pen, but rather I was someone learning, writing, and working right along with them. My realization of this change is captured best in Freire's noble words:

> The teacher is no longer merely the-one-who-teaches, but one who is himself taught in dialogue with the students, who in turn while being taught also teach. They become jointly responsible for a process in which all grow. (1970, 80)

As I reread these prophetic words, I recognize that daybooks were my way to create this *dialogue* for myself, my students, and our writing. In most classrooms, the teacher is traditionally perceived as the expert or supreme possessor of knowledge. And as much as I and many other idealistic teachers may try to level the playing field and counterbalance these roles, the reality is that they clearly exist. Through daybooks I found a way to break down some of those inevitable roles in the classroom.

I am continuing to explore other means of applying Freirean pedagogy within my classes, whether it is a critically reflective twist added to a normal, daily activity or a complete restructuring of my classroom environment. Whatever the outcome, I have begun to acknowledge and adopt the understanding that "knowledge emerges only through invention and reinvention, through the restless, impatient, continuing, hopeful inquiry human beings pursue in the world, with the world, and with each other" (Freire 1970, 72). Though this effort may prove frustrating at times, I have learned how important it is to continually bring awareness to my students, awareness of their writing and how their writing can affect their lives. For it is only through awareness that change can ultimately occur. Daybooks provide me and my students with a means to record and reflect on our ever-growing awareness, and they are the evidence of the change that has occurred over time.

Reflections on Getting the Daybook Started, One Step at a Time

Though we do have an entire chapter providing strategies on introducing the daybook (see Chapter 3), we want to share some of our personal reflections on the experience. Daybooks are students' tools for thinking. Their value becomes almost immediately apparent to the student, but their messiness can raise questions from those who haven't experienced the daybook's power. Now that we've given you the theoretical underpinnings for taking on such a project in your classroom and Shana has shown you what that critical theory looks like in a classroom, following are our stories of inspiration and starting places to remind you that all it takes is one step at a time. Listen to Tony's and Lil's stories as they navigated through some of the questions and complexities that arose when they first started using daybooks with their students.

Tony's Story: Ten Minutes to School Literacy

It is crucial to me that I establish a community within my classroom that respects students' expressive language. How do I show this respect to my students? It starts with the daybook. However, at first I had to figure out a way to get students comfortable writing in this new space because they were used to writing on loose-leaf paper that ultimately was turned into the teacher for a grade. I want my students to feel free to write as a way to share pieces of who they are with the class without worry of right and wrong or good and bad grades. To do this, I assign students ten minutes of nightly writing in their daybook. This assignment is called a freewrite, meaning that the child is free to write about whatever she desires. My only requirement is that she times herself by writing down the start and finish time of the freewrite. Students are welcome to continue what they've started the next morning in the classroom during an assignment I call *Writing into the day*. Here the child has another opportunity to express what is on her mind by starting a new thought or building off of the one from the previous night.

Before we start our writer's workshop each day, our designated time later in the day to work on more specific classwide writing assignments, I let the students share their freewrites from the night before to continue to foster the sense of community I am striving for. Each day students come to me in the morning after they've unpacked, excited to share what they've written the night before. I've seen a range of writing come out of these freewriting assignments—everything from Christmas wish lists to letters to family members, reflections on the day before, story starters, poems, you name it. Their language is full of life and is as diverse as the ethnicity of my students.

Despite the positive effects on school literacy I observe from implementing the ten-minute freewrite, some parents are disturbed by the idea of freewriting when they first see it. Like Shana's freshman composition students, they can't seem to keep themselves from editing grammar, punctuation, and spelling before the writing is turned into the teacher. At one of the first parent meetings of the year, I have to explain to parents the importance of the daybook and freewriting in the development of young writers and thinkers. I have to make them understand that students need to first be comfortable transferring thoughts to paper. Editing doesn't come until *much* later in the writing process, after students have mined the gold from their daybooks and picked ideas that will later turn into published pieces. I tell parents who want to help their students that the best thing they can do for this ten minutes of writing is be an interested audience by listening and asking questions about the ideas represented. For those who want to go one step further, I suggest that they get into the habit of keeping their own daybooks and freewrite with their children. At the end of the ten minutes, they can switch daybooks and share what they have discovered that evening.

Over the course of the school year, I notice that the ten-minute freewrites become more and more elaborate and sometimes longer. This is a result of the ongoing development of community within my classroom. Though the pressure from parents and schools to insist on correctness is strong, I resist the temptation to use what is easy—writing worksheets and fill-in-the-blank writing exercises. As a result, because my teaching values this seemingly random thinking that gets captured in the daybook, students and parents have learned to rethink what writing and literacy look like in the classroom. Taking the emphasis off things like length and correctness provides a place for growth in the classroom through sharing, editing, revision strategies, and writing workshops.

The ten-minute freewrite, a small and simple assignment, is my way to make the daybook a staple in my classroom. I want my students to know that freewriting, like the daybook, is an opportunity to be themselves on paper. There are days that I do not assign the ten-minute freewriting for homework. This always raises an eyebrow or two, and I'll hear, "Can we still write for homework even though you haven't assigned it tonight?" This usually results in a big smile on my face as I say, "Of course you can, and I can't wait to see what you write." Empowering students through a ten-minute freewrite for homework? Doesn't sound possible, you say? Come to my classroom sometime, ask my students if anyone's interested in sharing their work, and see what happens!

Lil's Story: Learning Takes Time

Just so no one gets the wrong idea: It took me several years to really make daybooks work. The first time I tried them was a total flop. I brought my daybook to class the first day, had the daybook listed on the syllabus as part of the requirements, and promised myself that I was going to really make this daybook happen in my classroom. My dedication lasted three weeks tops, but most likely two. Then the old binder-girl mentality took over, and my classroom returned to the olden days. At the end of the semester, when my students asked me, "So what are we doing, again, with these daybooks?" I felt guilty and depressed. I knew I had taught my students a lot. I just wasn't sure that they learned what I had taught.

So I changed to Plan B. I asked Karen, our super-organized coauthor, to team-teach with me one summer and show me how she implemented daybooks. Having Karen there with me made the daybooks come alive. I loved my daybook; our students loved their daybooks. The daybooks worked. Once the summer term ended, I knew the feeling I wanted in my classroom, but I also knew that I was more like Shana when it came to daybooks—organized chaos was much more my style.

I tried again the next semester. I started this time having my students write into the day, just like Tony has his young students do—I would take the first five minutes of class for everyone to open their daybooks and freewrite, just to collect their thoughts for class. Because the daybooks were open and thinking was happening right from the start, I was able to remember to have my students try out ideas, summarize our conversation, and define terms that we had been discussing. In other words, the daybooks started to become essential, a necessary part of our classroom conversation. I won't say that the binder girl has totally moved on—she emerges from time to time trying to take over or speed things up. But now I just tell her to open her daybook and write.

Spreading the Word in Schools

We have been so excited about how daybooks helped us enact our philosophy of teaching in our own classrooms that we couldn't wait to share the ideas with our colleagues. This has taken time and patience on our parts. Stories like Lil's and Tony's remind us of what it takes to get started and the length of our own journeys. Are you the only person in your school who would even consider deviating from script, formula, pacing guide, or whatever it is that limits students' thinking in your school? Are you frustrated to find yourself in that position? We've been there too. Following are stories of inspiration for those of you who feel alone. Something as powerful as the daybook can not go ignored forever.

Cindy's Story: Let the Students' Work Speak for Itself

After falling in love with the daybook as a graduate student, I was hired at the largest high school in North Carolina as a tenth-grade English teacher with the responsibility, much like Karen, to help with writing. The department head knew of my involvement with the National Writing Project and my past success with the North Carolina Writing Test. The scores for the school the year before had kept them from meeting their goals, so all eyes were on me. I ignored the eyes and began using the daybook with my six classes of regular tenth-grade English students. Early in the year I did a workshop on daybooks for the school, and while teachers were interested, they were too busy to try anything new. The real selling point for daybooks at my school was the students.

A group from the English department met daily in my room to eat lunch at the desks where my students left their daybooks. With permission from my students, they began to flip through them. First, they noticed the glued in handouts and the sheer number of pages the students were writing. They started asking questions and the daybooks began to be referred to as "Cindy's little books." One colleague and dear friend became so interested in them that she began to experiment on her own with her regular level English class. Because of the new-found freedom her students felt, the daybooks were a hit.

I went on maternity leave the following year, and my friend came to my house before school started to have a crash course in setting up the daybook and to read all of the research I had to support what I was doing with them. It turned out that she had many of the same students I had taught the year before and their first question to her was, "Can we keep using our daybooks?"

Because I found myself without a permanent classroom when I returned from maternity leave, I always invited the teachers whose rooms I was floating into to stay and work during my classes, and they saw my students using daybooks. Again, the students' engagement with their writing and thinking intrigued my colleagues, and they began to ask questions.

In the end, the students have been the catalyst for the spread of the daybook at my high school, not test scores or my workshops. As the years have gone by and students have come and gone, the daybook is the tool that they have carried with them. I am proud to say that my colleagues have come to recognize the value of a tool valued by students and have worked to make it work in their classrooms as well.

Karen's Story: The Literacy Broadcast

After figuring out how to use my own daybook and one with my fifth-grade class, I became a literacy coach in a Title I elementary school. Just like Cindy, I first was brought in to help with writing. As I entered my new position, I naturally began thinking about how I could integrate the use of daybooks. I asked myself, "Could I take daybooks schoolwide?"

I talked with the principal, Kelly Propst, and explained daybooks. She liked the idea, and through a combination of school funding, class supply lists, and my own personal gifts, we worked to get a daybook into the hands of each third-, fourth-, and fifth-grade child in the school because those were the grades I worked with primarily. I began going from teacher to teacher and classroom to classroom introducing daybooks and integrating them into the upper grades. A buzz started in the school, and the teachers and grades I did not work with regularly wanted to know what these daybooks were all about. Like all teachers and literacy coaches, my time was limited, so I had to figure out a way to spread the word as quickly and efficiently as possible, so to further illustrate daybooks to teachers and students, I started videotaping the students I had been working with, explaining how they wrote in and used them. I showed the three-to-four-minute videos on closed-circuit TV each Friday morning to a school of 750 students and staff.

Television worked! Seeing others talk about their daybooks intrigued teachers and students, and did far more justice to the daybook much faster than any presentation or workshop I might have given. Like Cindy, the students' experiences with daybooks was powerful!

At my school, children now walk the halls with their daybooks and eagerly share their writing with teachers. Our halls are walking galleries of posted student work. In most classrooms, there is an author's chair where students share their work and listen to their classmates' critiques. An "author wall of fame" bulletin board is in the front lobby. Every year we boast a winner or two in the state Young Author's Contest. It is obvious that we emphasize writing and writing to learn at our school through daily instruction, our Friday "Literacy Broadcast: Where Kids Teach Kids to Write," contests, and a yearly evening coffeehouse for authors and their parents in November. Within three years, we have gone from a school that needs help with writing to a nationally recognized Title I school.

What Students Say About Their Daybooks

After all that we have said about daybooks, it's only right we give our students a voice as well. We would never have learned what we have learned about daybooks without our students. Nothing inspires us more to roll up our sleeves and get to work than the resounding amens of our students. Here's what they have to say!

Daybooks Make Writing, Thinking, and Learning Enjoyable
It feels good to have a daybook because you're not forced to use one topic.
You can make up your own topic and use your own words. My daybook

*helps me learn because I like to look back and read my stories.
If you do daybooks, you should have a share time. Reading stories from
my daybook to friends also helps me find mistakes. A daybook is something
you can keep forever! When I'm twenty-eight years old, I'll probably
still have my daybook.*
—ELEMENTARY STUDENT

*Daybooks have inspired me to write more and more. Daybooks have also
helped me enjoy writing. I think that all new teachers should know that you
can always keep your ideas of topics that you want to write about in your
daybooks. And you can write funny, sad, happy, silly, or any kind of writing
in your daybooks. I have mostly stories I made up in my daybook but I have
other things, too, like stories that I glued in and lots of main topics and
little topics that are specific. Like I might have holiday and maybe
Christmas under it. And I also keep a topic list where I keep
the ideas for things I'd like to write about.*
—ELEMENTARY STUDENT

*I like my daybook because I can write whatever I want in it.
It helped me tell about things I am feeling. I like to write in
my daybook when I have free time.*
—ELEMENTARY STUDENT

I like my daybook so I can write amazing things.
—ELEMENTARY STUDENT

*I like daybooks because you can feel passionate about what you write
about and doesn't matter if it's a good story or a bad story; it matters if
you care and if you put your best effort to it. It's like my own diary.
My own space where I can feel free to write.*
—ELEMENTARY STUDENT

*I try to make it really pretty. I like to make it creative and colorful because
then I'm actually interested in learning. I know that if it's in here, it's
important and it's not going to get lost.*
—HIGH SCHOOL STUDENT

Daybooks Help Generate Ideas and Thinking

*I like my daybook because we get to write anything we want. The daybook
has helped me because it gives me ideas. You can share anything you want. I*

think daybooks could be better with more and more people writing in the daybook as the years go by. Because more people are learning more.
—ELEMENTARY STUDENT

It helps me calm down. I write my thoughts and my questions. My stories, my poems. I like to write my settings, my writing entries. My daybook helps me think.
—ELEMENTARY STUDENT

I use my daybook for everything really, including my math homework, but mostly I just like to write my pieces in it and it's a good place for me to think and brainstorm my ideas.
—HIGH SCHOOL STUDENT

Daybooks are a curious phenomena. On one hand, they are merely composition notebooks and yet, they are so much more. They are like a literary porthole to your soul, an eternal abyss with the potential to encapsulate the plethora of thoughts that emanate from the mind of the student. Daybooks UMMM, lovey dovey!
—HIGH SCHOOL STUDENT

Daybooks Keep Us Organized

I like my daybook because the pages don't come out. You get a binder and the rings get all messed up and then the pages fall out. I can keep all of my literary stuff in it. It's really organized because everything stays in one place.
—HIGH SCHOOL STUDENT

I use my daybook for everything in English class and it's really good because everything's in one place—all of the writing about books and all of the papers we do. It's great because I can look back and reference the ideas—I can find ideas for big papers easily.
—HIGH SCHOOL STUDENT

Daybooks Rock!

From the student who is incapable of keeping track of her papers, daybooks are wonderful. Everything you need for that class is there, in one notebook. No searching random papers in a messy notebook, because it is all combined and simple. The benefit of having everything you need for a class is obvious, but even more daybooks allow students to really process, digest if

you will, information. After writing down enough random stuff, it starts to
get useful. The daybook serves as the ultimate reference/practice tool.
Anytime I need to think of ideas or need a direction on how to approach an
in-depth novel study, I can just go back in my daybook for help. English
class is like everything else—practice makes perfect—and the daybook
is the perfect place for this to occur.
—HIGH SCHOOL STUDENT

Now What?

Our greatest advice is to start. Start with yourself. Begin writing and figuring out what you want to write and how you write. How does a daybook fit into your teaching and writing life? Then, share your ideas with your class. Test your theories about what will work with them. Engage them in the study. Ask them to talk about and write about what's working and what needs work. If daybooks improve writing in your classroom, step out and share with your grade level or department. Then maybe go schoolwide by showing students on closed-circuit television teaching one another or hold open workshops for teachers and students.

Set a small goal. Meet it. Set the next. You may be pleasantly surprised by the ownership students feel and the enthusiasm for writing they display months later in your daybook project. You will witness that all of you relax. You relax because you don't have to read and grade everything for students to become better writers, and your students relax because they won't have you constantly looking over their shoulders. You both will have the freedom to explore and then display your best which is a much more natural way of learning any new process. And then some day you may receive an email like the one below, from a student who has gone on to bigger things.

In every English class I'd taken prior to yours, we always wrote to a formula, analyzed literature to a formula, and basically thought to a formula. We rarely did anything that required any real original thought and creativity on the part of the student, and while I was pretty good at it, it was boring and tedious. Before I took your class sophomore year, I hadn't learned any real writing or reading strategies that were useful beyond the specific assignment they were intended for.

But, upon taking your class for two years, I learned a whole new way of approaching writing and reading. It became more about what the student thought about a piece of literature rather than what a textbook told us to think. I remember very few, if any, days where you told us what to think. You always provided the springboard for thought, but all the actual thought was ours. After a while, that critical thinking about our reading and writing became second nature. Eventually, we didn't need to do reading responses, etc. any more because you had trained us to think that way automatically. Looking back, I loved your classes because I felt that I had really done something, like I had learned something that I could apply later in my educational career. (By the way, I still freewrite before I write a paper.) I was proud of the work I did because the thoughts behind it were mine, and not someone else's. I kept my daybooks and all the papers I wrote for that very reason. And even now, some two-odd years later, I still look back at them when I get stuck on an assignment. Even if the actual material in the daybooks or the papers isn't relevant anymore, the strategies behind the thoughts in the daybooks still are. If I've learned anything in college, it's that I can still write (take a multiple choice test, not so much the same story . . .).

REFERENCES

Allen, Janet. 1999. *Words, Words, Words: Teaching Vocabulary in Grades 4–12*. Portland, ME: Stenhouse.

Atwell, Nancy. 1987. *In the Middle: Writing, Reading, and Learning with Adolescents*. Portsmouth, NH: Boynton/Cook.

———. 2002. *Lessons That Change Writers*. Portsmouth, NH: Heinemann.

Bakhtin, Mikhail. M. 1981. *The Dialogic Imagination*. Austin: University of Texas Press.

Berthoff, Ann. 1981. *The Making of Meaning*. Portsmouth, NH: Boynton/Cook.

Brandt, Deborah. 1998. "Sponsors of Literacy." *CCC* 49 (2): 165–183.

Britton, James. 1980. "Shaping at the Point of Utterance." In *Reinventing the Rhetorical Tradition*, edited by Aviva Freedman, Ian Pringle. Conway, AR: L & S Books, for the Canadian Council of Teachers of English.

———. 1982. *Prospect and Retrospect*. Portsmouth, NH: Boynton/Cook.

———. 1983. "Language and Learning Across the Curriculum." In *Forum: Essays on Theory and Practice in the Teaching of Writing*, edited by Patricia L. Stock. Portsmouth, NH: Boynton/Cook.

———. 1993. *Language and Learning*. Portsmouth, NH: Boynton/Cook.

Britton, James, Tony Burgess, Nancy Martin, Alex McLeod, and Harold Rosen. 1975. *The Development of Writing Abilities*. London: Macmillan.

Burke, Jim. 2007. *The Teacher's Daybook, 2007–2008: Time to Teach, Time to Learn, Time to Live*. Portsmouth, NH: Heinemann.

Burns, Olive Ann. 1984. *Cold Sassy Tree*. New York: Bantam/Dell.

Cobb, Vicki. 2005. *Harry Houdini: A Photographic Story of a Life*. New York: DK Publishing.

Colegate, Isabel. 2007. www.quoteworld.org/quotes/2965. Accessed 14 May 2007.

Daniels, Harvey. 2002. *Literature Circles: Voice and Choice in Book Clubs and Reading Groups*. Portland, ME: Stenhouse.

Dr. Who. 2007. www.quotationspage.com/quote/1460.html. Accessed 14 May 2007.

Druker, Peter. 2007. www.brainyquote.com/quotes/quotes/p/peterdruck165702.html. Accessed 17 May 2007.

Elbow, Peter. 1996. "Writing Assessment: Do It Better; Do It Less." In *Assessment of Writing: Politics, Policies, Practices*, edited by Edward White, William Lutz, and Sandra Kamusikiri. New York: MLA.

Esquivel, Laura. 1999. *Like Water for Chocolate*. New York: Doubleday.

Fitzgerald, F. Scott. 1991. *The Great Gatsby*. New York: Cambridge Univ. Press.

Fletcher, Ralph. 1996. *Breathing In, Breathing Out: Keeping a Writer's Notebook*. Portsmouth, NH: Heinemann.

Fox, Mem. 1998. Personal Conversation. Whole Language Umbrella Conference, Charlotte, NC.

Freire, Paulo. 1970. *Pedagogy of the Oppressed*. Trans. Myra Bergman Ramos. New York: Herder & Herder.

Goswami, Dixie, and Peter Stillman, eds. 1986. *Reclaiming the Classroom: Teacher Research as an Agency for Change*. Portsmouth, NH: Boynton/Cook.

Grimes, Nikki. 1993. *Jazmin's Notebook*. New York: Dial.

Imbrie, Ann. 1999. "Words Become Us." *Vassar Quarterly* 96 (1): 14–19.

Jewitt, Carey. 2003. "Re-thinking Assessment: Multimodality, Literacy and Computer Mediated Learning." *Assessment in Education* 10 (1): 83–102.

Jewitt, Carey, and Gunther R. Kress. 2003. *Multimodal Literacy*. Bonn, Germany: Peter Lang.

Johnson, Samuel. 2007. www.quoteworld.org/quotes/7253. Accessed 14 May 2007.

Johnston, Peter. 1997. *Knowing Literacy: Constructive Literacy Assessment*. Portland, ME: Stenhouse.

Kalmikoff, Jeffrey. 2006. *Designing for Community with Zero Advertising Brands*. Austin, TX: South by Southwest (SXSW).

Knoblauch, Cy, and Lil Brannon. 1984. *Rhetorical Traditions and the Teaching of Writing*. Portsmouth, NH: Boynton/Cook.

————. 1988. "Knowing Our Knowledge: A Phenomenological Basis for Teacher Research." *Audits of Meaning: A Festschrift in Honor of Ann E. Berthoff*. Portsmouth, NH: Heinemann.

Macrorie, Ken. 1985. *Telling Writing*. Portsmouth, NH: Boynton/Cook.

Marklin, Jeanie, and Shana Woodward. 2006. "Do the D.E.W.: Discover and Empower Through Writing." *North Carolina English Teacher* 62 (1): 28–31.

Martin, Nancy, Pat D'Arcy, Bryon Newton, and Robert Parker. 1983. *Writing and Learning Across the Curriculum 11–16*. London: Ward Lock.

McBride, James.1996. *The Color of Water: A Black Man's Tribute to His White Mother*. New York: Riverhead.

Murray, Donald. 1982. *Expect the Unexpected: Teaching Myself—and Others to Read and Write*. Portsmouth, NH: Boynton/Cook.

————. 1986. "One Writer's Secrets." *College Composition and Communication* 37 (2): 146–153.

————. 1990. *Shoptalk: Learning to Write with Writers*. Portsmouth, NH: Boynton/Cook.

Rief, Linda. 2003. *100 Quickwrites*. New York: Scholastic.

Romano, Tom. 1995. *Writing with Passion: Life Stories, Multiple Genres*. Portsmouth, NH: Boynton/Cook.

————. 2000. *Blending Genre, Altering Style: Writing Multigenre Papers*. Portsmouth, NH: Boynton/Cook.

————. 2004. *Crafting Authentic Voice*. Portsmouth, NH: Boynton/Cook.

Rose, Mike. 1980. "Rigid Rules, Inflexible Plans, and the Stifling of Language: A Cognitivist Analysis of Writer's Block." *College Composition and Communication* 31 (4): 389–401.

Rosenblatt, Louise. 1978. *The Reader, the Text, the Poem: The Transactional Theory of the Literary Work*. Carbondale: Southern Illinois University Press.

Selfe, Cynthia. 1999. *Technology and Literacy in the Twenty-First Century: The Importance of Paying Attention*. Carbondale: Southern Illinois University Press.

Smagorinsky, Peter. 2001. *Teaching English Through Principled Practice*. New York: Prentice-Hall.

Spinelli, Jerry. 1990. *Maniac Magee*. Boston: Little, Brown.

Tzu, Sun. 1983. *The Art of War*. New York: Delacorte Press.

Urbanski, Cynthia D. 2006a. "The Daybook Defense. Assessing Writers' Notebooks Without Valuing Product Over Process." *North Carolina English Teacher* 62 (1): 6–10.

———. 2006b. *Using the Workshop Approach in the High School English Classroom*. Thousand Oaks, CA: Corwin Press.

Von Braun, Wernher. 2007. www.quotiki.com/quote.aspx?id=9811. Accessed 17 May 2007.

Vygotsky, Lev S. 1978. *Mind in Society: The Development of Higher Psychological Processes*. Cambridge, MA: Harvard University Press.

Weaver, Constance. 1996. *Teaching Grammar in Context*. Portsmouth, NH: Boynton/Cook.